Play Together Grow Together

A Cooperative Curriculum For Teachers of Young Children

Marilyn Segal, Ph.D.
Don Adcock, Ph.D.

Research and development for the revised and expanded version of *Play Together, Grow Together* was supported through a grant from the A.L. Mailman Family Foundation.

Play Together Grow Together

A Cooperative Curriculum
For Teachers
of Young Children

Dedication

In memory of my father, Abraham L. Mailman, whose commitment to caring and sharing has crossed the generations.

—Dr. Marilyn Segal

Acknowledgements

This revised and expanded version of *Play Together, Grow Together* is in every sense of the phrase a cooperative venture. Wendy Masi, Patti Lieberman and Becky Raitt played the roles of critics and collaborators. They raked through the manuscript with a fine toothed comb, weeded out overelaborate activities, and added playful ideas. Ann Miller played the role of project manager. She masterminded the production process, transferred revisions from scribbled notes to type set, set up photo shoots and kept us in range of a time line. The staff and students from Nova University's Family Center played the role of field testers. They tried out each activity, shared their certainty, and reaffirmed our belief in the value of cooperative play.

ISBN 1-879744-03-1

51295>

9 781879 744035

New Edition

Cover Art and Design:
Nova University, University Relations and Development, Office of Publications

CONTENTS

INTRODUCTION

"Mine!" shouted Marianna, clinging to the arms of a stuffed toy rabbit. "Mine!" shouted Samantha in an even louder voice as she pulled on the rabbit's leg. Recognizing that young children have trouble sharing, the teacher assistant rushed to the other side of the classroom to find another stuffed animal. When she returned with the toy, she was surprised to find Marianna and Samantha playing happily together. Samantha was holding one arm of the rabbit and Marianna was holding the other. "Swinging, swinging," chanted the girls as the bunny flew through the air.

The ability of young children to play together, and even negotiate conflict, has received considerable attention among child development experts. In earlier literature the play of young children was described as parallel, side by side play with no interaction. The way to keep the peace in preschools was to provide several duplicates of the more desirable toys. Recent studies of young children at play have contributed new insights. Very young children are often socially quite sophisticated, sharing toys and ideas and negotiating conflicts so that each child ends up happier. Furthermore, longitudinal studies where children have been followed from preschool to grade school have demonstrated that the achievement of social skills in preschool is associated with success in school as measured by both social and academic performance.

While young children have the capacity to cooperate and negotiate simple conflicts, this capacity is not always reflected in their behavior. The development of social skills in preschool requires careful monitoring and ongoing support. A skillful teacher must be on hand not only to help negotiate the inevitable conflicts, but also to help children develop a repertoire of social skills. In the course of the preschool years, children have many social skills that they must acquire: how to gain entry into a play group; how to cope with rejection or exclusion; how to be appropriately assertive; how to share, take turns, and recognize different perspectives; how to generate compromises; and how to initiate and maintain friendships.

While most preschool teachers support the concept of building social skills, developing a classroom that optimizes social growth requires a rethinking of many accepted practices. This is particularly true when we

Developing a classroom that optimizes social growth requires a rethinking of many accepted practices.

take a close look at techniques teachers use to motivate appropriate behavior. How often have we heard teachers use the following phrases:

"Who will be the first one to put the toys away?"

"Suzie is sitting quietly, so she gets to lead the lunch line."

"Abigail, I am so proud of you. You are my best helper."

Although none of these teachers is being inappropriate, the messages they are sending to the children are "be the fastest, be the first, and be the best."

Because competitive values are ingrained in our culture, it is not easy to implement a cooperative curriculum. It is particularly difficult when we recognize that a cooperative curriculum requires careful analysis of every facet of a child's learning experience: the materials and equipment that are placed in the classroom; the way the room is arranged; the content and context of the curriculum; the relationships with children, family, and community; the techniques used to motivate children; and the incorporation of cooperative goals into all classroom activities.

Play Together, Grow Together is a resource for teachers who are committed to a cooperative curriculum. It provides many different examples of cooperative activities and techniques that teachers can incorporate or adapt. Because it is organized in chapters according to type of activity, *Play Together, Grow Together* is well-adapted to an interest-centered classroom. At the same time, it can infuse a theme-based curriculum with cooperative ideas and values.

Chapters one through ten of *Play Together, Grow Together* are focused on a major curriculum area. The first section of each chapter describes concepts and skills within the curriculum area that foster cooperation. The second section presents examples inspired by classroom teachers of the cooperative ideas in action. The final chapter of *Play Together, Grow Together* provides guidelines and suggestions for fostering social skills. It is divided into three sections: reducing and resolving conflict situations, helping individual children who have problems with social skills, and enhancing prosocial behavior.

Throughout this curriculum guide, our premise is that giving preschool education a cooperative twist makes the experience more rewarding for both children and teachers. Children are stimulated to explore the aspect of school life that most appeals to them—the chance to play with others. And teachers are stimulated to focus on social growth, to respond when children need help building social skills, and to share with children and parents a commitment to cooperation.

Play Together, Grow Together *is a resource for teachers who are committed to a cooperative curriculum. . . giving preschool education a cooperative twist makes the experience more rewarding for both children and teachers.*

Chapter 1

DRAMATIC PLAY

Dramatic play is the hallmark of a cooperative curriculum. In a classroom that is organized in interest centers, make-believe centers are certain to buzz with activity. In the housekeeping area, a family of children has claimed squatter's rights. The mother is standing at the sink washing dishes and doling out jobs to her sometimes cooperative and sometimes stubborn children. In the doctor's office two children are standing face to face trying to negotiate roles. In the dress-up area three children have decided to enter the Olympics and are fitting themselves out with over-sized tee shirts and socks.

Dramatic play is the hallmark of a cooperative curriculum.

While almost every preschool includes a dramatic play center, the way the center is organized varies from classroom to classroom. In some classrooms the dramatic play area consists of a sink, a stove, a refrigerator, and perhaps a kitchen cabinet and a table with a couple of chairs. In contrast to the classroom we have just described, in many traditional preschool classrooms teachers maintain the housekeeping corner as their one-and-only place for pretending. In this situation, it is not uncommon to see this area taken over by a small group of children who have established themselves as a family. When new children attempt to enter the area, they are promptly ordered away by the family of self-proclaimed landlords.

Recognizing that the traditional housekeeping area can encourage exclusion, teachers who are interested in cooperation expand the scope of the playhouse. The teacher's goal is to find ways for more children to enter the play without losing the high level of cooperation that exists within a pretend family. This is not an easy task, but the tactic we suggest is to create a second imaginative play area right next to the playhouse. In other words, build a place for neighbors. Every few weeks the materials in this neighbor play area can be changed to encourage a different kind of imaginary theme. For two or three weeks the neighbor area could be a grocery store, then the play might be changed to a restaurant or a fire station. The neighbor area in one classroom we visited was a puppet theater. The theater was positioned so that it could be seen from the playhouse sink and stove. As the family members pretended to wash the dishes or prepare a meal, other children used the puppets to talk to them.

Neighbors do not duplicate the pretend family in the playhouse, they complement it. Each time a new kind of neighbor is established, new possibilities open up for the family members. Members of the family can dash out to do their shopping, talk to the puppets next door, or call for a fireman. In the process, other children in the classroom are included in the imaginary play. The playhouse remains the center of the action, while a number of new themes and a cast of new characters revolve around it.

Although teachers can set up a new neighbor play area and hope that the children will find it, it is usually better to introduce the new area during group time. Teachers can show the props to the children and talk about how they are used for pretending. Books related to the theme can be read, or perhaps a relevant field trip can be planned. Introducing the neighbor theme in these ways enables teachers to demonstrate new play ideas and explain new rules more efficiently.

Variations

The Neighborhood Area concept suggests endless variations. The selected scene can reflect an upcoming holiday, a costume shop for Halloween, a gift wrap and mailing station for winter holidays, or a card shop for Valentine's Day. In classrooms that use a theme of the month approach, the neighborhood area can reflect the selected theme. If the theme is community helpers, a post office could be set up. If the theme is a visit to the zoo, set up a gift store that sells "zoo" items. If the theme is growing things, set up a flower shop with plastic or child-made flowers. A third type of area that works well in some classrooms is "Grandmother's House." In a classroom where more than one culture is represented, Grandmother's House can include artifacts, crafts, clothing, games, kitchen utensils, and play foods that represent the culture of some children in the class. This idea works best when families are invited to the classroom to help set up the area.

The Grocery Store as a Next-Door Neighbor

The Scene

A partially enclosed area is set up next to the playhouse. It includes: a large, low table (the checkout stand), a cash register or cash box, a calculator, play money and poker chips, purses and wallets, "Special" signs, a variety of coupons cut from newspapers, pencils and shopping-list pads, large and small grocery bags, a telephone, a scale, shopping baskets, strollers or wagons, a sign that says "Open" on one side and "Closed" on the other, shelves stocked with empty food boxes, egg crates, soap cartons, plastic bottles, and other items found in a grocery store.

A Sample Script

This is the opening day for the grocery store, and about ten children eagerly converge on the scene. A dominant girl takes control of the cash box and starts doling out money to her friends. Anticipating a problem, the teacher points out that there is plenty of money for everyone in a cash box on her desk. "That is the bank," she explains. "If you need money to go shopping, you can get it there. The money box in the store is for giving out change."

Several children claim the wagon and shopping basket and start to load them with food. Within minutes they have filled their carts to the brim and are lining up at the checkout stand. Other children, holding a few items in their hands, are already checking out. "Would you like to be the 'bagger'?" the teacher asks a boy who is standing near the cashier, wistfully eyeing the cashier's prestigious position. The boy bags while the girl pretends to add up the items on the calculator. Some of the younger children, unwilling to wait, bag their own groceries and leave without paying.

Ten minutes later the crowd has thinned out. The grocery store is nearly empty, except for some merchandise that litters the floor. The teacher shows the cashier the "Closed" sign and suggests that it is time to close the store until it is restocked. Gathering together several younger children, she models the role of the stocker. The group collects food from around the room and puts it back on the shelves. "Store's open, store's open," the cashier calls out, as she props up the "Open" sign.

Opportunities for Cooperation

Initially, things may be quite chaotic in the store. During this time the teachers's role is to keep the play from bogging down in conflict. A second source of money keeps the cashier from playing favorites or hoarding all the cash. If the cashier's job is coveted by several children, the teacher can suggest other jobs, such as bagging, weighing, or answering the telephone, while the children wait their turn to be cashier. Both enthusiasm and cooperation are heightened when large props are used. A large shopping basket enables friends to shop together; large bags encourage group bagging.

As the novelty of the store diminishes, children will shop more leisurely, and the cooperative play will be more coherent. Children from the playhouse may shop for the family dinner. Children from the block area may buy food for a picnic. At this point the teacher will have a chance to help children fill in any steps in the sequence of shopping that they are

Both enthusiasm and cooperation are heightened when large props are used. A large shopping basket enables friends to shop together; large sacks encourage group bagging.

overlooking. The step that is most difficult, and generally requires some teacher help, is restocking the shelves. Unless the grocery store keeps receiving food as well as selling it, the play will break down. In this regard the "Open/Closed" sign is very useful. It helps the children remember that a store must be ready for business before it is opened.

The Restaurant as a Next-Door Neighbor

The Scene

A partially enclosed area is set up next to the playhouse. It includes: a long counter with several cash boxes, play money, paper sacks, straws, and empty catsup and mustard bottles; paper and pencil; napkins; food trays; menus or a blackboard with chalk; a small table with props for making hamburgers (red Play-Doh, rolling pins, circular cutters—tin cans or cookie cutters, and buns cut out of cardboard); a salt shaker filled with salt; a small table with props for making drinks (plastic cups, a plastic bucket of ice cubes, a pitcher of water, squeeze bottles of diluted food coloring); a small table with props for making french fries (yellow Play-Doh, a salt shaker filled with salt, several table knives, and cups for fries); several small tables for customers.

A Sample Script

"Hey, teacher, what kind of store is this?" asks one of the children in a group that is milling around the counter. "It's a fast food restaurant, like McDonald's or Burger King," the teacher replies. "Oh, great," a boy shouts in jubilation, "I love McDonald's."

"Wendy's is better," a girl states authoritatively. "Well," interjects the teacher, "this is a pretend restaurant, so it can be part McDonald's and part Wendy's." With a bit of instruction from the teacher, the children are soon busy making hamburger patties, cutting Play-Doh snakes into french fries, and pouring cold drinks.

The teacher models the role of customer by standing at the counter and calling out her order. She encourages the children to use labels like "customer" and "worker" in order to make the distinction clearer. Additional children are drawn into the play by being asked if they want to order too, and the teacher helps them elaborate their orders by asking questions like,

"Do you want your food to go or are you going to stay in the restaurant?" "Did you want to order a large coke or a small one?" These remarks are not lost on the workers. As the next customer approaches, the girl behind the counter says briskly "Is this to stay or to go?"

Opportunities for Cooperation

As in the case of most imaginary play in the classroom, cooperation first takes the form of imitative manipulation. The children are absorbed in manipulating the props, rolling out the Play-Doh, cutting it with cans and blunt knives, mixing water of different colors, and putting food into hamburger boxes. Gradually, those who are most interested in the theme settle into imaginary roles.

A boss may emerge among the workers in the kitchen. In fact, this is a natural role for the mother in the playhouse to adopt. In general, the role of customer is not as powerful or desirable as the worker roles. The teacher can jazz up the customer role with creative suggestions. For example, the teacher might model the idea of taking a doll to the restaurant for a meal; or the teacher might suggest that a customer buy a surprise meal for other children in the room and then deliver it to them.

Variation

Instead of being an imaginary eatery, the place next door to the playhouse can become a Play-Doh bakery or, even more simply, a table. A Play-Doh table, like a water table, stimulates relaxed, parallel play. The essential ingredients, besides the Play-Doh, are instruments to manipulate it, such as rolling pins, cookie cutters or blunt knives, and containers, such as pie plates, muffin tins, cookie sheets, and Jello molds. Changing the instruments and containers from time to time will, of course, make the play more lively.

In addition, teachers can encourage children to experiment with different decorating ideas. Play-Doh products can be sprinkled with coarse salt or glitter; they can be drawn on with Magic Markers; they can be topped with shaving cream. Tinker toy sticks, large beads, or pieces of costume jewelry can be placed strategically in a cake, a cookie, or a pizza. The process of creating new accessories and decorations for Play-Doh products makes the play more exciting and more cooperative.

Occasionally children will also get involved in a grandiose joint project, such as making a very long snake or making all the letters of the alphabet. Although such moments are relatively rare, teachers certainly will want to support this kind of effort.

Cooperation in most imaginative play areas begins with imitative manipulation. Gradually, children become interested in a theme and settle into imaginary roles.

The Fire Station as a Next-Door Neighbor

The Scene

A partially enclosed area has been set up next to the playhouse. It includes: a small table and chairs, a long hose (coiled up), several sleeping bags or cots, blankets, several fire hats, a telephone, a bell on a nearby shelf, a stretcher, several empty soda cans, a lunch box, play food, a box of dominoes, and a first-aid kit (Bandaid box, bandages, a sling).

A Sample Script

"Is this a fire station?" asks a boy as he tries on a fire hat. "Yes," answers the teacher. "But where are our masks?" the boy demands. "We can't breathe smoke, you know."

"Well," the teacher replies, "I guess you'll just have to pretend."

"And why are these beds here anyway?" the boy remarks in a critical tone.

"So you can sleep at the fire station," the teacher explains. "Firemen have to stay all night at the fire station in case there is a fire."

At this point the teacher is interrupted by persistent clanging. One of the boys has discovered the fire bell and has taken it off the shelf. "Be careful over there," the teacher insists. "That's the fire alarm. When someone reports a fire, they ring the bell. Then you wake up and put out the fire."

"Yea," says another boy, "with this hose. Here, help me pull it out. Boy! It's really long." The group of boys uncoils the hose and discovers that it reaches to the other end of the room. "Do you have anything on fire?" the teacher asks the children in the playhouse. "There are some firemen in the neighborhood now and they can help you."

"Yes," the mother of the family reports, "our stove is on fire."

"I'll just ring the alarm," the teacher says. She rings the bell until the firemen, who now number four, have noticed the sound and rushed over. "Quick," the teacher shouts, "the stove is on fire in that house."

"Pull the hose in here, men," the leader of the boys commands. The mother of the family graciously invites the firemen to stay for coffee after the fire is put out, but the chief declines gruffly "We're too busy now—but we'll come back later."

Opportunities for Cooperation

The fire station represents a playhouse with extra appeal for boys. At the station they can eat their meals, sleep, and do many of the everyday things that occur in the regular playhouse. The teacher can reinforce the similarity between these two play areas by suggesting that the firemen borrow materials from the family in the playhouse. Perhaps they can borrow some plates, pans, or pillows. Or perhaps they can even ask the children in the playhouse to deliver meals to them. In return, the firemen can help the playhouse children by putting out fires.

The long, heavy hose encourages cooperative fire fighting. A fire truck, whether mobile or stationary, tends to create fights because each of the children wants to drive. Better to rush to the fire by unwinding and pulling the hose. The beds or sleeping bags help extend the play by giving the firemen something to do between fires. An element of suspense is added as the firemen close their eyes and wait for someone to ring the bell. This alarm bell, which serves to organize play, gives shy or unattached children a chance to participate. They can ring the bell, and even if the alarm is initially a false one, someone will most likely find a fire to put out.

Sooner or later there will be pretend casualties in these fires. Preschool children are well aware of the terrifying possibilities of being burned up. Since combustion is such a mysterious process, it makes sense to the children that the medical treatment for burns be magical too. The teacher might suggest that the firemen carry victims back to the station and then use a short hose to spray them with a special burn medicine.

Preschool children are frequently intrigued by the way a fire gets started. A popular theme, which promotes cooperative firefighting, is that some evil force or thing keeps starting fires in the classroom. The firemen may try to track down a malevolent insect, such as a fire spider, or some ever-present but invisible fire monster.

The Emergency Room

The Scene

The playhouse has been moved into the center of the room and arranged so that it can be entered from all four sides. On one side of the playhouse is an imaginary ambulance, complete with a steering-wheel toy, walkie talkies, and a blanket for a stretcher. On the opposite side is what looks like an operating table. In another part of the room there is a combination doctor's office/hospital room with a bathroom scale, a number line (in inches) for measuring height, and a bed with a tray. The play store in the classroom has become a pharmacy. In each of these areas there is a doctor's kit and a few pieces of specialized equipment.

The doctor's kit contains: a stethoscope, shot needles, a flashlight, cotton balls and masking tape (for bandages), tongue depressors, and medicine bottles.

Specialized equipment includes: a diploma; a rubber knife and large plastic needles (for operations); a black box with two tin cans attached to the sides by electrical wire (for starting a heartbeat); white jackets, masks, and rubber gloves; blankets and towels; Ace Bandages and slings; plastic medicine bottles and spoons; prescription pads and pencils; and a plastic catsup bottle with a hose attached to the top (for giving blood transfusions).

A Sample Script

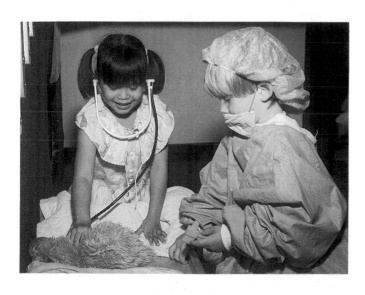

The children fan out quickly across the room and soon are playing in pairs and threesomes. One child stands on the scale, while a second child administers a shot and dabs the immunized spot with a cotton ball. Another pair is involved in a makeshift operation. The patient lies on the operating table while the doctor pretends to mend a broken arm. The doctor presses a flashlight against the arm, makes a buzzing noise and says, "Now I made you a bionic arm." Still another pair is sitting at the steering-wheel toy. They pretend to drive somewhere, making siren noises and talking excitedly into their walkie-talkies. The play episodes are short and disjointed.

Two girls who usually play in the playhouse approach the doctor's office. "My daughter is sick," the older girl says to the doctor. "I guess she'll have to go to the hospital," the doctor replies, motioning with his arm toward the nearby cot. The mother helps cover her daughter with a blanket and then watches as the doctor puts his stethoscope on the girl's forehead. "She has lots of germs," he pronounces authoritatively. "She will have to stay here three weeks." The "sick" girl giggles quietly to herself. In a matter of minutes the three weeks pass, and the mother takes her daughter home. In just a few more minutes she is back with another family member who needs to be hospitalized.

As the family members take turns going to the hospital, a boy rushes into the playhouse, announces loudly that he is dead, and then collapses dramatically on the floor. The teacher directs the attention of the driving pair to this catastrophe. "Hey, ambulance drivers, someone just died over there. Better get him to the doctor." In due course the victim is carried and dragged to the operating table.

Several doctors converge on the scene. "What happened to him?" the teacher asks. After some discussion the doctors agree that the boy was shot. "Looks pretty serious," the teacher agrees as she picks up the empty catsup bottle. "Maybe he needs some more blood." She inverts the bottle and touches the attached tube to the patient's arm.

The doctors poke and probe the patient with their operating tools. "I think he's alive now," one of them finally says. "No, I'm still dead," the patient insists. "What do you do with dead people?" the teacher wonders. "Let's throw him in the river," suggests a doctor. Unable to cure their patient, the doctors and ambulance drivers haul him away to the river. But as they struggle to dispose of the corpse, it scrambles back to life and runs away laughing, "I'm O.K., I'm O.K."

Opportunities for Cooperation

In this example the teacher intentionally went beyond the usual scope of neighbor play. Instead of creating a second imaginative play area adjacent to the playhouse, the playhouse was moved to the middle of the room and then medical play areas were grouped around it. As the center of attention, the playhouse was more vulnerable to intrusion. But at the same time, outlying play areas helped balance the exposure of the play-house. While new children entered the playhouse, such as the child who "died," the regular family members were being drawn to the hospital, one of the peripheral play areas. This kind of radical change in the classroom environment would not work all the time but, used occasionally, it is an exciting way to reinforce imaginative play and open up the playhouse to additional children.

When the neighbor theme is doctor play, the highest level of interaction is associated with medical emergencies. The process of bringing victims to the doctor's office or the hospital for operations, transfusions, and heart resuscitation easily becomes a group project. Preschool children whose pretending is advanced will be quick to pick up these themes. Other children will gravitate toward the more mundane medical instruments seen in everyday office visits. They will look at throats and ears, give shots, and perhaps use a bit of tape as a Bandaid. These children are more likely to play in pairs.

Whether the doctor play is simple or complex, a potential stumbling block to cooperation is finding a willing patient. With pairs, the teacher can suggest that the children take turns being the sick person. Or both children can be the doctor while a doll is the patient. With a larger group, the teacher can suggest that emergency patients are victims of glamorous accidents, such as crashing in a race car or getting in a fight with a bear. As in our script, someone frequently "dies" spontaneously in the classroom and can be recruited for the patient role.

Instead of creating a second imaginative play area adjacent to the playhouse, the playhouse was moved to the middle of the room and then medical play areas were grouped around it.

THE BLOCK PLAY AREA

Organizing Ideas

Young children are capable of building extensive, even intricate, structures with blocks. Surprisingly, very little block building takes place in many preschool classrooms. Building with blocks at school is different from building at home because the balance between construction and destruction is altered. In a classroom situation, children who work together to make a block structure are far outnumbered by the other children who could pass by and destroy it. These children do not have a stake in the construction, and the temptation to be destructive is almost irresistible. Even if a block structure survives the pillages of the peer group, it subsequently falls prey to clean-up time.

Because block structures are so difficult to preserve, the block corner in a preschool classroom may not be a popular spot. Of course, a few children who are really intrigued with block building can be found there. These "master builders" frequently adopt an autocratic approach to block play. They seem bent on creating a separate world under their exclusive control. Children who are less committed to block play are not about to challenge the self-appointed kings of the block area.

In order to encourage more of the children to share in the joy of block building, teachers need to find a variety of ways to make the block corner attractive. Ideas that have worked well for some teachers include the following:

1. Change the look of the block area on a regular basis by adding interesting props.
2. If your classroom uses a thematic approach, set out props in the block area that encourage thematic play:
   - If your theme is transportation, put out cars, trucks, and long blocks. Children will use the blocks to create roads and bridges or tunnels.
   - If your theme is a farm, put out a variety of small animals with smaller long blocks that can be used as fences.
   - If your theme is the water, put out large hollow blocks, paddles, fishing rods, and empty cans so that the children can build a fishing boat.

Building with blocks at school is different from building at home because the balance between construction and destruction is altered.

Another way to call attention to the blocks is to take them off the shelves before the children come to school. The teacher can begin a structure of some kind, or better yet simply stack the blocks in a big pile. When the children arrive, the teacher might say something like:

> I left the blocks out today because I wanted to see what you could build. If you build something special, come and tell me about it. We will leave all the buildings up until the end of the day. Then we will clean up the block corner.

From time to time teachers can go further and actually get involved in block building. When teachers join in block play, their goal is not so much to demonstrate new ways of building, but to help children coordinate the building skills they already possess. These group building efforts under the direction of the teacher can stimulate a broader level of participation and cooperation, even if sometimes they do not represent the ordered, stable world sought by the "master builder" type.

Space is an important factor in block play. Cooperative building takes more space, and the best kind of blocks for joint projects are large, hollow, wood blocks that take a great deal of space. Even when children build independently with smaller blocks, they need enough space to stay out of each other's way. In classrooms that are lacking in space, the teacher can make the block corner expandable. The shelves or dividers that define the block corner can be combined with another area on special days when the teacher wants to emphasize cooperative block play.

If a classroom can afford them, large, hollow, wood blocks are ideal for cooperative play. With these blocks, children can build houses big enough to get inside. They can build child-sized boats and airplanes. The blocks are so heavy, and the building scale so large, that joint efforts are almost inevitable. Many preschools substitute large cardboard blocks because they are less expensive. These blocks are good for cooperative tower building, but they are too light for making stable platforms, enclosures, or tunnels.

The most common blocks in preschool are kindergarten or unit blocks. These blocks can be used for large-scale cooperative projects, like an amusement park or a network of roads. More often kindergarten blocks are used to build structures of moderate size. This means that there is room for only two or three children to work at the same time. In these circumstances, cooperation is best extended by encouraging other small groups of children to undertake similar projects. Several towers, castles, or houses may spring up in the same vicinity, and if toy vehicles are handy, the children probably will visit each other by driving back and forth between their constructions.

Group building efforts under the direction of the teacher can stimulate a broader level of participation and cooperation.

Tower Building

The Scene

The teacher is building with a large set of red, cardboard blocks (each block is about the size of a shoebox).

A Sample Script

"What are you doing, Teacher?" a boy asks as he watches the teacher place several cardboard blocks against a wall in the block corner. "I'm making a chimney; want to help me?" the teacher answers. "Sure," the boy cheerfully responds. Soon three other children have joined the project. The design of the chimney is very simple: Each layer is constructed with three blocks in a U shaped pattern, with the open part of the U facing the wall.

As they work the teacher talks to the children about bricklaying. "These bricks won't hurt if you drop them," one of the builders remarks, dropping the block on his foot to illustrate his point. A rash of brick dropping follows. Seeing that the children are getting wilder, the teacher says, "It would be really easy to knock over this chimney because our bricks are so light...but let's see how high we can build it." The children get interested in measuring the height of the chimney against their bodies. Quickly the chimney grows from being waist high to eye level to above the children's heads. The children stand back to admire their achievement, but after just a few moments of reflection, the urge to knock down the tower becomes overwhelming.

A couple of the original builders, with a new helper or two, begin to rebuild the chimney. This time someone has a new idea. "Let's put toys in the chimney," a girl suggests. "It will be a Christmas chimney," the teacher adds, following up on the girl's suggestion. When the chimney, which is about three feet tall, has been filled with toys from around the room, the children decide to cover the top with blocks. "Let's open it up," the girl proposes, and again the destructive impulses of the group come to the fore.

"This time I'm going to hide inside," a boy announces, "cover me up." Amidst confusion, the building commences once more.

Opportunities for Cooperation

The key to cooperative tower building is to get beyond a minimum height. Once a tower gains enough height, the children want to maintain the tower's balance, and they add new blocks carefully. In this example the teacher initially did three things that helped the tower reach the critical height. First, she participated in the building herself. Second, she started the tower against a wall. (The support of a wall makes a tower much more stable.) And third, she gave the block building an imaginary context—the tower became an imaginary chimney. Tower building may evolve in different directions. One possibility is to build higher and higher towers. In our example the teacher expanded this idea by helping the children measure themselves against the tower. Another possibility is to build hollow towers and fill them. Young children generally build solid towers but then discover that some interesting holes have appeared inside. By starting a hollow tower, the teacher creates an interesting hole in the beginning. Objects can be placed inside the tower and the tower built around them, or objects can be dropped inside the tower after it is finished. An exciting object to enclose, in the minds of many children, is themselves.

When children build a tower, the most likely outcome is building a tower and then knocking it down. This too can be a form of cooperation, if it does not endanger the participants, damage the blocks, or disturb the play of other children.

Pens and Fortresses

The Scene

The following items are placed in the block play area: a set of kindergarten blocks, and a plentiful collection of toy animals, vehicles, or miniature characters.

A Sample Script

A rectangular structure with three cows inside has been placed in front of the block area. "Look, it's a farm," a boy exclaims. "Let's build a farmhouse." He and a friend start to construct a square building near the animal pen. As soon as the four walls have been completed, the boys put two horses in their farmhouse. Apparently the farmers on this farm are horses.

On the other side of the pen three younger children have built an adjoining corral and filled it with several pigs and a spotted cow. They are pretending that the animals know how to jump from one pen to the other. Sometimes these acrobatic animals jump on top of the fence and do a balancing act.

Meanwhile the two boys are adding a roof to their farmhouse. Soon the horses disappear from view, completely enclosed in blocks. The boys make the walls thicker by adding a second layer of blocks. The farmhouse looks impenetrable. "We need a secret door," one of the boys says to his friend.

Opportunities for Cooperation

In this example, the teacher has stimulated enclosure building by making a large animal pen before class began. Several younger children construct one small pen. Then they lose interest in building. They are more interested in moving the animals in and out of the pens. The two older boys create a more complex enclosure—a kind of fortress for their horses.

Building pens and fortresses is a flexible theme with many variations. Generally, however, two principles will become evident: (1) a pen needs to have something in it, and (2) the purpose of the pen is to protect whatever is inside. The more avid builders will make their pens increasingly isolated and fortified. Cooperative building tends to be limited to two children who can enjoy the pleasures of companionship but still feel in control of their property. On the other hand, a group of children who are less absorbed in building may peacefully share a large open enclosure, using it to develop imaginary play.

Platform Play

The Scene

A wooden frame, approximately 33" x 33" made out of 2x4s, is set up in the block play area. Props include: a set of kindergarten blocks and a collection of cars, trucks, and airplanes.

A Sample Script

"Who will help me fill this frame with blocks?" the teacher asks. "We've got so many spaces to fill up," she remarks to several children who begin to help her. The frame has been constructed so that it matches the dimensions of the kindergarten block. The children use about 30 blocks of different sizes before the frame is completely filled in. "Now we have a platform," explains the teacher. "It is nice and solid and won't fall apart." A boy steps on top of the platform and jumps up and down just to test the teacher's point.

"What shall we do with our platform?" the teacher muses. "It looks kind of like a parking lot or maybe an airport."

"Or a skating rink," offers a girl who is fond of ice skating. "Let's make it into a house," a dominant boy suggests. Soon walls have sprung up around the platform, but when the children try to step in the house, the sides topple over. "I'm making a garage," says another boy. He builds a garage next to one side of the platform and puts a truck inside it. Other garages appear across the perimeter. Trucks from the garages are pushed onto the platform.

Someone takes out a few blocks, creating a square hole in the platform. "That looks like a lake," the teacher comments. The lake quickly expands until it is big enough for the trucks to drive in. "My truck goes in water... So does mine...I'm looking for fish." Little blocks (representing fish) are loaded onto the trucks and the drivers head back to their garages, presumably to eat in private.

Opportunities for Cooperation

The wooden frame promotes cooperative building in two ways. First, it provides a common reference point for the group. Part of the structure is in a sense pre-planned, which gives the group a good start toward further planning. Second, the filled-in frame provides a durable base, one that will not come apart as the group builds. Whatever kind of superstructure the children build on top of or around, the platform is likely to fall down in time, but the foundation will remain intact. The more stable the foundation, the more likely the children are to rebuild.

The most common superstructure is a house. However, the foundation of the home is especially suited to transportation play. By removing some of the blocks, a network of roads appears. By leaving the blocks in place, the solid platform becomes an arena for demolition derbies, a launching pad for rockets, or simply a plaza for neighbors to congregate with their vehicles. Like the group in our script, the children may build dwellings around the edges of the platform and then drive from one dwelling to another. The presence of the platform stimulates their natural tendency to visit each other.

Ramps and Tunnels

The Scene

The following props are placed in the block play area: a set of kindergarten blocks, several 1" x 8" boards four feet long, and a collection of small cars and trucks.

A Sample Script

In front of the block shelf, a stack of blocks is holding up one end of a 1" x 8" board to create a ramp. Several racing cars have been placed beside the ramp. As soon as free play starts, two boys discover the ramp, with the cars and trucks parked underneath. They immediately begin to roll the vehicles down the ramp. Sometimes, however, the cars do not roll straight, which causes them to plunge off the side of the ramp prematurely. "I'm building a wall," one boy proposes. He lines his side of the ramp with blocks. The second boy follows suit and constructs a wall along the other side. Meanwhile the teacher shows some other children how to build a road at the end of the ramp. By now there is a group of six children at the ramp. Cars and trucks are going up and down in confusion.

"Watch out! The wall is breaking," shouts one of the boys. A large truck has just careened off the side of the ramp. The partial collapse only stimulates further destruction. Several cars accidentally—or on purpose—demolish the rest of the wall. "We don't need this," another child asserts as she swings a long block and systematically knocks the other wall off the ramp. "Let's use these blocks to make the road longer," the teacher comments cheerfully. Her hopeful mood is picked up by one of the players. "Let's build the road all the way to the windows," he says to the others.

Opportunities for Cooperation

Rolling cars down a ramp (or propelling them up a ramp) is exciting to young children and is likely to draw a crowd. However, the end of the trip is somewhat of a letdown. The car speeds down (or up) the ramp and then stops. Occasionally it crashes in an interesting way, and invariably some of the children concentrate on creating more and more spectacular crashes. The children cooperate in this enterprise, at least to the point of admiring each other's daredevil driving. In most cases, the wildness that this kind of play stimulates is vented in acts of destructiveness. The ramp, the road, whatever is built with the blocks, is not destined to last very long. The play runs in cycles of construction and destruction. The teacher can lengthen the

Rolling cars down a ramp (or propelling them up a ramp) is exciting to young children and is likely to draw a crowd.

cycles of construction by helping the children create side trips and destinations. A tunnel at the end of the ramp, a parking lot or garage along the road—spots like these give added purpose to the play and put off for a bit the inevitable doomsday. When the destruction does come, the teacher can accept it calmly and wait patiently for another constructive impulse from the children. Then she may want to help clear away the rubble and assist in the rebuilding.

City Blocks

The Scene

Four rolls of brown wrapping paper (approximately 3' wide and 4' long) are lying rolled up on the floor. The rolls are lined up end to end, with an 18" space between rolls. One end of each roll has been tucked under the block shelves. Since one end of each roll is effectively anchored, the children can unroll the paper and create four distinct building areas. As the teacher describes it, the four squares of paper are city blocks, and the spaces in between them are the streets.

A Sample Script

"Hey, you're on my property," a boy building on one of the city blocks yells at his neighbor. "Yeh, that's right," the boy's partner chimes in. The neighbor's foot has inadvertently trespassed while its owner was concentrating on the completion of a tall building. Silently the offending neighbor acknowledges his error and pulls his foot back onto his own city block. He is a talented builder and likes to work by himself. The other two boys, who seem so concerned about property rights, are making a crude racetrack on their paper.

Gradually a third, and then a fourth square, are unrolled and used for block play. For the most part the children play independently. "Hey, you can't drive your truck there," the bossy boy yells again. This time his neighbor is pushing a dump truck down the aisle between the two papers. By way of explanation the boy adds, "That's a river—it's not a road."

"Let's make a bridge," suggests his partner, who is more mild-mannered. The boy driving the truck likes this idea too, and all three boys cooperate in building a bridge that links the two city blocks. Having finished the bridge, the truck driver goes back to driving. "My truck can go in water," he maintains stubbornly as he ignores the bridge and pushes his truck down the aisle.

Using paper squares to define separate building areas helps a group of children coexist in the block corner.

Opportunities for Cooperation

Using paper squares to define separate building areas helps a group of children coexist in the block corner. Although the children usually build independently, especially in the beginning, they are attentive toward each other. Not only do they watch for violations of their space, they observe the different kinds of structures that are built. And because arguments over space and unintentional acts of destruction are reduced, these block structures tend to be more elaborate than in an undefined block corner.

SENSORY ACTIVITIES

Organizing Ideas

Sensory play is an important ingredient of a cooperative curriculum. While splashing and pouring water, sifting sand, or shaping a handful of clay, children engage in casual conversation. They are enjoying being together and have no concerns about taking the lead or playing one-upmanship. Children who are not quite sure whether to risk an entree into an established play group can always retreat safely into the sensory center. Sensory bins can be filled with different materials: cornmeal, colored rice, macaroni, mud, feathers, beans, or oatmeal.

Water play has great appeal whether you are a child, adolescent, or adult. Sometimes water becomes an exhilarating medium for play, from the mild splashing and squirting of preschool youngsters to the water balloon fights of older children to the fire hose battles of college students. Much of the time, however, water has just the opposite effect. It soothes and calms. In the classroom, water play occurs most often at a water table, and in this situation wildness is ruled out. Water play is by necessity restricted to the quiet mode. When a water table activity is working, the pace slows down and the interaction mellows.

If a classroom cannot afford a commercially made water table, a plastic wading pool or plastic trays from the grocery store may be used instead. The favorite activity for quiet water play is pouring water. Every conceivable container is filled and emptied—plastic butter tubs, coffee pots, funnels, jars of all sizes, squeeze bottles, medicine droppers, cans with holes punched in them. By using their ingenuity, teachers discover containers they had never before considered. One teacher, for example, discovered that a flour sifter made a wonderful water toy. The play potential of the water table is further enhanced if these pouring toys are changed on a regular basis. Then the children will continue to be surprised and captivated by their transformations of water volume.

Sand, like water, is a "feeling" experience. For preschool children, sand is above all something to be handled—to be sifted, poured, patted, and shaped. The finer the sand, the more pleasant these tactile sensations, and the more relaxed and calming the play.

Sensory play is an important ingredient of a cooperative curriculum.

A novel sensory experience brings children together to explore, experiment, and discover.

While outdoor sand play (described along with outdoor water play in chapter nine) lends itself to cooperative projects like building and baking, the cooperative element of an indoor sand table is likely to be shared conversation. At the same time, with the addition of appropriate props, cooperative projects can be initiated in the classroom sand bin.

In contrast to sand and water, clay is primarily an indoor activity. There are many different types of clay that can be used in preschools. Some types of clay, like peanut butter clay and "goop," are homemade, and preparation of the clay is an opportunity for cooperation. Other types of clay are prepackaged, and children cooperate in dividing up the clay or creating a cooperative product. Like sand and water, clay is an easy material to share, and the clay table is likely to be a place where children engage in casual conversation.

Sensory experiences involving tastes, scents, visual effects, and textures are likely to be special activities, introduced from time to time as a part of a curriculum unit. Bubble blowing may be introduced as a part of a unit on weather. Taste experiences may be introduced as a part of a unit on food, and a texture activity may be introduced as a part of a unit on clothes. Most teachers feel that there is an advantage to having some sensory activities that are a permanent part of the classroom and others that appear from time to time. A permanent sensory bin is a safe haven when children need soothing or relaxation. A novel sensory experience brings children together to explore, experiment, and discover.

Water Play

The Scene

A water table is set up in the classroom. A variety of containers has been placed on a nearby table—funnels, pitchers, sieves, plastic cups and glasses, measuring cups, plastic margarine containers, pint-size bottles, long handled spoons, and paper cups.

A Sample Script

One child is pouring water from the pint bottle into a funnel. "It's raining, it's pouring, the old man is—"

"I'm making rain, really, really," another child comments as she pours a cup of water through the sieve. "Why don't we make a hurricane?" suggests a third child, who has just joined the group. The children around the table accept the idea and the fine rain turns to torrents. When the children discover that splashing the water works even better than pouring, the teacher intervenes, "My goodness, I think we've had a long-enough hurricane. As a matter of fact we're having a flood. All hands out of the water, we have mopping to do."

Opportunities for Cooperation

The teacher can increase the level of cooperative play by introducing different props. The water play can be a baby doll bath, a lake for launching boats, or a diving pool for miniature Disney World characters. Another possibility would be a fishing trip, using a tray of ice cubes as fish and some fishing nets.

Sand Play - A Dinosaur Egg Hunt

The Scene

A sand table is set up with shovels, spoons, and small spades. Before class, the teacher has buried twelve plastic eggs underneath the sand. Twelve miniature dinosaurs have been lined up on a nearby table.

A Sample Script

Because of a traveling dinosaur exhibit at the local museum, the teacher has decided to do a curriculum unit on dinosaurs. During circle time, the teacher plays a lotto game with the children, which involves matching miniature dinosaurs with some dinosaur picture cards. At the end of circle time, the teacher tells the children that there are some special dinosaurs around the room. There is a dinosaur activity set up in the art corner, some dinosaur books in the language area, and, "you know what else? Some dinosaur have laid their eggs in the sand table."

A half dozen children hurry to the sand table. "Do you think there really are dinosaur eggs in the sand box?" one child asks. "Of course not, you silly, dinosaurs are extinct."

"They are not stinked," another child insists, "cause my daddy saw real footprints when he went to Arizona."

"I found one, I found a dinosaur egg," one child shouts excitedly, as she pulls a plastic egg out of the sand. "No fair, that was my spot. That dinosaur belongs to me—" The teacher interrupts, "There are plenty more dinosaur eggs in the sand. As a matter of fact, there are twelve dinosaur eggs in the sand and twelve dinosaurs are lined up on the table. See if you can find an egg for every one of the dinosaurs."

Opportunities for Cooperation

Treasure hunts are always popular with children. When the goal of the treasure hunt is to see who can find the most treasure, the hunt becomes competitive and all but one child become losers. When the goal of the hunt is to find all of the treasure, the hunt becomes cooperative and everyone wins together.

Clay - The Goopy Experience

The Scene

Four children are sitting around a small table manipulating a "goop" ball. The goop, which the class has helped to make in the morning, is made from 1/2 cup laundry starch and 1/2 to 3/4 cup school glue. It has been left in a plastic baggie for an hour in order to let it harden.

A Sample Script

"This stuff feels awful, it's goopy, goopy, goopy."
"Hey, I'll take your piece, I like the way it feels."

"Well you can't have it cause I'm making doo doo." The children start giggling. "I'm making doo doo too. Doo-too-poo, I made a rhyme."

"Look at mine, I made a ball and it bounces."

"Doo-doo-doo-doo look I made rabbit ears."

Opportunities for Cooperation

Despite the steady flow of conversation, these children are not talking together. Each child is manipulating a piece of "goop" and pretty much doing his own thing. But despite the fact that the children are not working on a joint project, or even imitating each other, the activity is cooperative. The children are sitting peacefully at the table, sharing ideas in a casual way and enjoying each other's company. Cooperation does not necessarily mean that children must collaborate.

Blowing Bubbles

The Scene

Bubble-blowing props are added to the water table. They include: dish detergent, 18" lengths of garden hose, straws, plastic bowls and glasses of different sizes, diluted food coloring in plastic squeeze bottles, and plastic tubes. Sponge mops and a bucket are set aside until later.

A Sample Script

Lying in the water table are half-a-dozen pieces of garden hose. The water looks clear enough, but several tablespoons of dish detergent have been added. The children fish out the hoses and begin to experiment with them. Some try to capture water in the hoses and pour it out; some try to use them like blowguns. "Remember to blow out," the teacher warns as children pick up the end of a garden hose. In a few minutes, all have found out that the most-fun thing to do is to blow bubbles in the water. The soapy bubbles boil up in mountainous forms. One of the children discovers she can make a funny noise by pursing her lips and blowing through the hose like a trumpet. Other children try to imitate her. The bubble making gets noisier as children toot and hum through their hoses. As the children play, they talk briefly about the nature of the bubbles—how they stick together, how they pop, how they sometimes spin. But the group seems most bent on covering the surface of the water with bubbles. Whenever an open spot appears, it is attacked by the bubble makers.

Opportunities for Cooperation

This activity generally does not involve much organized cooperation, but it produces a happy group feeling. In the background there is a sense that something is being done that is just a little naughty. All those noises and bubbles are not usually allowed. After the children have had ample opportunity to experiment with bubble blowing, the teacher might introduce a new play theme, such as Dairy Queen. Plastic bowls and glasses of different sizes can be added, and the children can use straws to blow bubbles in these containers. Depending on the experience of the children, the bubble concoctions can be ice cream cones, floats, or sundaes. And they can be made fancier by adding diluted food coloring. Advanced pretenders may even try to sell their ice cream wares to other children in the classroom. At the end of the water play, children are encouraged to engage in cooperative clean up, with some children scooping up the bubbles and putting them in a bucket and other children drying the floor with the sponge mop.

Variation

Give the children bubble-blowing wands and let them blow bubbles into the air. Imitative and cooperative activities will spontaneously materialize, such as chasing the bubbles as they sail away, trying to catch them before they touch the ground, or trying to catch two bubbles at the same time.

The Perfume Factory

The Scene

A table has been set up with the following items on it: several small pitchers of water, one large jar, one-dozen baby-food jars (without lids), stirring sticks, plastic squeeze bottles full of colored water that is mixed with perfume ingredients, such as: syrup, cooking oil, cologne, vanilla extract, cinnamon, mint, Worcestershire sauce, vinegar, etc.

A Sample Script

During free play, a group of children is introduced to the perfume factory, which is set up near the water table. "See all these bottles?" the teacher says. "Everyone of them has a special smell inside it. Here, smell this one." The teacher waves the syrup and water bottle under the noses of the children. "What's that smell like?" she asks them. "It's something you put on pancakes."

"Syrup!" a girl shouts out. "Right," the teacher replies, "but it doesn't taste very good because it's mixed with water."

At the end of the water play, children are encouraged to engage in cooperative clean up, with some children scooping up the bubbles and putting them in a bucket and other children drying the floor with the sponge mop.

"We can use these bottles to make our own perfume," the teacher continues, demonstrating how to mix the ingredients in a baby-food jar. "My mother gets mad at me when I play with perfume," another girl remarks in a serious tone. "But," responds the teacher, "I don't think she'll be mad if you play with this pretend perfume, do you?"

"No, I guess that's alright," the girl concedes.

The children begin to work intently on their own mixtures, occasionally letting out an exclamation of excitement or offering their neighbors a whiff. The teacher notices that the younger children keep adding liquid to their baby-food jars even when the jar is overflowing. "Here," she says to one child, "you can pour the full bottle in this big jar and then start over. That way we can save all our perfume."

Opportunities for Cooperation

Most children will make their own individual bottles of perfume, but by providing a large jar the teacher encourages communal perfume making as well. After filling a small jar, the children usually are willing to add their perfume to the large jar, and some children may eventually work directly on filling this larger container. The communal perfume can be used at a later point in time. It might be transferred to a squeeze bottle and then applied to dolls. It might serve as after shave lotion when children pretend to shave. It might be poured back into little bottles and taken home by the children. The salient point, which can be emphasized by the teacher, is that the perfume was made by everyone.

ART ACTIVITIES

Organizing Ideas

Art is an avenue for expressing individuality, but art activities can also provide a way to work together. Artists, whether young or old, use their art to express their own unique way of perceiving and interpreting experience. In the art area there is no right or wrong way of creating a product, and there is no place for competition. At the same time, art activities provide children with a special opportunity to share their thoughts and ideas. With the help of the teacher, children discover ways of putting together their individual work to create a collaborative project.

Several techniques for stimulating cooperative art are outlined on the following pages. These techniques include both free form activities and projects built around ready-made forms. Young children respond positively to both approaches, and both are valid. Artistic expression can be involved in decorating a preconstructed form as well as in creating an original one. Free-form arts and crafts have the advantage of remaining simple and spontaneous. When teachers provide young children with ready-made forms, or when they expect children to create a particular form, there is always a danger that the activity will require too much teacher direction. In an activity undertaken by a group, this adult direction can interfere with peer interaction and eliminate much of the cooperation that might otherwise take place.

Not all arts and crafts activities can be, or should be, cooperative efforts. Children enjoy doing their own work and should not be denied the pride of individual workmanship. But even when an art activity is designed for individual participation, the products can become part of a cooperative venture. A room can be decorated with butterflies or flowers that have been created by individual children. Individual paper chains can be combined to form a class chain. A "gallery" wall can be set aside where children tape up the art work they would like to share with their peers. A mural can be created to illustrate a favorite story or portray the theme of the week.

On the one hand, art is a creative endeavor, reflecting originality, independence, and divergent thinking. On the other hand, it serves to unite people, to help them build a common world view. Young children

Art is an avenue for expressing individuality, but art activities can also provide a way to work together.

enjoy both these characteristics of art work. They like to pursue their own artistic idea and have it admired by others. When children see their individual work becoming part of a classroom creation, they experience the joy of creativity and the power of collaboration. The art activities that are described here can be repeated throughout the year, with or without elaboration. Some of the activities lend themselves well to particular themes or units. We describe a city sculpture, for instance, that can be a part of a unit on the city, a unit on trees, or a unit on building. Other activities, like a "creative" collage, can be used at any time during the year or adapted to any unit.

City Sculpture

When children see their individual work becoming part of a classroom creation, they experience the joy of creativity and the power of collaboration.

This scene is introduced as a part of a unit on The City We Live In. A low table is set up in the classroom. One chair is placed on each side of the table. Props include: a 2' x 2' square of plywood with several large blocks of wood glued on it, a box full of smaller wood blocks and chips, and white glue.

A Sample Script

It is morning circle time, and the teacher is talking about the plywood square, which is in front of the children. "Look at this, I started making it last night. I thought I would make a city. First I glued this big block here, and I decided it was the bank. Then I wanted to make a telephone office building, so I glued this block. Then I decided I would bring the city to school and see if some children wanted to help me finish it. What else do you think this city needs?" Gradually the children think of answers: houses, hamburger places, a bakery, a bus station, a junkyard, grocery stores.

The teacher explains that the plywood base and the box of wood scraps will be left on a nearby table, so that during free play children can work together to build the city

Later in the morning, the teacher hears a commotion near the new project. "I was here first," one boy protests. "Well, I want the glue now," a second boy demands. "You can't help us," a third boy threatens. Arriving on the scene, the teacher points out that there are four chairs around the table. "Remember," she reminds them, "in our room the chairs show us how many children can play at the same time." At the teacher's request, each boy takes a seat. "Three boys in three seats," the teacher muses, "that leaves one seat for me." The teacher admires what the children have built and asks them what they will work on next. Then she comments, "I think I'll decorate the bank. I'll put some little blocks on the top—you know, like signs."

Opportunities for Cooperation

Glueing wood scraps is a favorite art activity with preschool children. The basic forms already exist, but the children can create a great variety of structures by combining them in different ways. Since the most common construction is a house or building, the teacher thought a whole city would be a good cooperative project.

Realizing that the interaction between builders would be more manageable if the group were small, the teacher set a limit of four children. She noted that the children had followed her lead by glueing separate, large blocks on the plywood base. She introduced a new idea by decorating one of the buildings with small wood scraps. The teacher might have suggested other new ideas, like bridges between buildings, sidewalks, a park, or a junkyard where irregular shapes would predominate. These suggestions do not necessarily give the city a realistic look, but they help the children use the wood scraps more creatively.

During the initial phase of building, the teacher can occasionally bring the city to circle time and talk to the children about it. "What was built yesterday? What can be added to the city?" When the buildings are complete, the teacher can periodically bring the city out and encourage the children to decorate. "It's getting to be wintertime," the teacher might say, "What can we do to decorate our city?" The city might be covered in cotton snow, draped with holiday decorations, or populated with miniature people and animals. On Valentine's day, the city could be festooned with Valentine cards that the children cut out and paste on the buildings. Spring might bring a new coat of paint to the city. Such renovation and beautification projects, of course, will probably be teacher ideas.

Two Colors are Better Than One

The Scene

A low table is set up in the art area with room for four children to sit or stand. Props include: several large sheets of fingerpaint paper and fingerpaints in at least four colors.

A Sample Script

The teacher enlists the aid of some children as he tapes the sheets of paper on a low table. "Are we going to color?" one of the children asks. "Even better than that," the teacher responds, "We are going to paint with our fingers."

"Oh goody, fingerpainting," a nearby child squeals as she joins the group at the table. "Today," the teacher continues, "every-

Mixing colors, an
exciting activity for
preschool children,
invites cooperation.

body gets a chance to paint with a friend." The teacher shows the children what he means by arranging the children in pairs, facing each other across the table. The teacher then offers the children on one side of the table a choice between yellow and green fingerpaint. The children across from them get a choice of red or blue. This means that each pair of children who share a paper has two different colors of fingerpaint. "Wait a minute," the teacher announces, "I'm going to put on the special, super dooper fingerpainting music guaranteed to make your fingers dance or your money back."

The music begins, "I got yellow, I got yellow, it's so yellow," the squealer hums. Across from her, a sober boy pushes his blue fingerpaint around with deliberation. Little by little, the two colors approach each other, the blue making short, crooked jabs, the yellow sweeping in wide circles. "Hey, your yellow is in my way," the boy complains. "So what?" the girl blithely replies, "My yellow can go anywhere."

"And look what happened," the teacher remarks. "When your yellow ran into his blue, they both turned green. It's like your yellow seeds plus his blue water made green grass. Now you have three colors." The girl looks briefly at the teacher, as if to see whether his crazy analogy means he is really crazy. Then she addresses the boy, "Let's make lots of green."

"O.K.," the boy answers at once.

Opportunities for Cooperation

Mixing colors, an exciting activity for preschool children, invites cooperation. In our example, the teacher structured this cooperation by putting children on opposite sides of the table and giving them different colors. The interaction would have been more intense, and the mixing experiments more surprising, if the teacher had used one sheet of paper to a table and positioned four children at the table with four different colors.

Although young children enjoy mixing colors, they do not always welcome encroachment on their side of the paper. When starting the activity, the teacher might wish to draw a circle for each child and place the fingerpaint inside this circle. The circle becomes the exclusive painting territory for that child, but whenever the child strays outside the circle, neutral territory is entered, and color mixing is in order.

If children enjoy sharing a finger painting activity, experiment with joint projects. Try spreading a large sheet of paper on the table. Give each of the children at the table a different color of paint. You could make the activity even more exciting by placing "toppings" on a nearby table that all the children can share—seeds, oatmeal, coarse salt, glitter. Whatever the final product, the children will enjoy the process of working together.

Paper Maché

The Scene

Prior to class, the teacher creates a simple playhouse made from cardboard cartons. Two sides from one carton form a peaked roof. The roof is attached to a second carton that serves as the main floor of the house. Doors large enough to crawl through and several windows are cut in this carton. The gables of the house are filled in with triangular pieces of cardboard left over from the first carton. Props include: a bucket full of paper maché (strips of newspaper soaked in a flour and water mixture) and a parent volunteer.

A Sample Script

It is free-play time, and the children are involved in their usual pursuits. Without calling attention to herself, the parent volunteer starts applying a layer of paper maché to the cardboard house. Gradually, a few children notice this mysterious construction project and gather to watch. The parent invites them to help, but states that there is room for only three helpers at a time.

As they work, they talk about paper maché. The parent explains that eventually it will get dry and hard, which will make the house more solid and make the walls stronger.

"This stuff is a kind of cement, isn't it?" one of the children says. "Well, sort of," the parent replies. "I think it will look more like stucco." This comment leads to a difficult conversation about the difference between cement and stucco.

After about ten minutes, the three children drift away to wash their hands and play elsewhere. The parent continues working at a leisurely pace, watching the children move around the room and waiting patiently for more helpers to show up.

Opportunities for Cooperation

Paper maché activities represent long term projects for preschool children. The buildup of paper maché is tedious, each thin strip of paper adding little to the overall form. The form itself may look misshapen, even unrecognizable, until it dries and is painted. This drying process means still more delay before the final product can be admired and used. At the same time, paper maché has an immediate appeal for young children. They are curious about the slippery paper. They want to touch it, and they wonder what makes it stick.

With these thoughts in mind, the teacher in our example has arranged for a parent volunteer to take responsibility for the paper maché playhouse. An adult is needed who can oversee and guide the first attempts of the

Paper maché has an immediate appeal for young children. They are curious about the slippery paper. They want to touch it, and they wonder what makes it stick.

children to work with this medium. The teacher and the parent expect these first attempts to be both enthusiastic and sloppy and, therefore, set a limit of three helpers at any one time. An adult also is needed to carry the project to completion, to provide continuity between the bursts of help from different children. The parent understands that cooperative work on the playhouse will be sporadic, and that the children may not appreciate what they have accomplished as a group until the project is completed.

Once preschool children become familiar with paper maché, a project can be approached differently. The children in the class who most enjoy this kind of craft activity can take a direct role in planning and carrying out the project. They have a better idea of what is involved, and they can be expected to stick with each phase of the job until it is done. The adult's role also changes. In our example, the parent volunteer began to work by herself and waited for the children to express interest. With children who are more knowledgeable, the adult's role is to organize and maintain a group effort among the children who participate.

Cardboard boxes provide a simple and sturdy material for a paper maché substructure. They lend themselves to houses of all kinds, but other forms come to mind as well. A single box might become a paper maché head, or on a more elaborate level, cardboard tubes could be added to create animals and robots.

A Creative Collage

The Scene

A collection of pictures of faces has been set in the center of the art table. Props include: a poster-board circle (about 15" in diameter), magazine pictures of faces, glue, and scissors.

A Sample Script

The teacher sees some children looking through the pictures that have been placed on the art table. There are about 30 pictures of faces; all ages, races, and expressions. "Do you want to make a picture with all these faces?" the teacher asks the children. They nod affirmatively and give her an expectant look. "Well," the teacher says, "Here is a circle we can use for the background. We will paste the faces on it and make a big, big crowd of faces." The teacher helps them get started. She explains that when people are in a crowd, they sometimes get in each other's way. "It's O.K. if one face gets on top of another; in fact, it makes the picture more interesting. See here, this little boy is hiding behind this old man." The children paste diligently for several minutes. "Teacher," a quiet girl asks, "can we cut too?"

"Sure," the teacher answers. "Would you like to cut the pictures and then paste them on?" The teacher demonstrates by cutting out a big eye and pasting it on the picture. "Some eyes are big and some are little, huh?" the quiet girl observes.

Opportunities for Cooperation

Collages represent an art form that appeals to quiet children who like to cut and paste. Doing the collage as a group has a distinct advantage in that a rich, detailed product can be assembled in a relatively short time. When doing individual collages, preschool children sometimes lose interest before they reach a point where the visual complexity of the collage becomes interesting.

Not only does a group effort bring a collage to fruition more quickly, but it invariably includes different perspectives and ideas. The creativity of the children is compounded when they work together. The teacher used a circular board so that the children added faces from different angles. The teacher also encouraged visual complexity by letting the children cut up the magazine pictures and add parts of faces to the collage. In the end, the group created a unique sea of faces.

Group collages can be structured in different ways. One way, which is illustrated in our example, is to give children a category of pictures such as faces, animals, food, clothes, or toys. These pictures, intact or in pieces, can be pasted on a circular background, or the teacher can further stretch the imagination of the children by suggesting a visual metaphor. For example, the background for a collage of car pictures might be a tree shape, and the teacher would introduce the project as a "tree of cars." On Thanksgiving, a food collage might be created on a silhouette of a turkey called a "turkey of food," as if the turkey had hatched a Thanksgiving feast.

Instead of creating a collage with overlapping images, the pictures can be distributed across a background. For example, the teacher might tape a long sheet of paper on the wall (perhaps 6' long) and paint or paste background pictures on it: mountain scenes, pictures of the sky, farm fields, etc. Then the children could complete the collage by pasting animal pictures on this outdoor background. The final product would be an artistic and imaginary natural environment.

The role of the teacher in collage activities is to help the children focus their attention on the arrangement of the pictures. The activity becomes interesting and results in more interaction as the children take the time to look at the pictures they are adding and the effect that is created. Just pasting the pictures willy-nilly on a background is neither cooperative nor artistic. The emphasis on composition becomes more feasible when the teacher cuts out the magazine pictures ahead of time. Then the teacher can

Collages represent an art form that appeals to quiet children who like to cut and paste. Doing the collage as a group has a distinct advantage in that a rich, detailed product can be assembled in a relatively short time.

spend her energy asking the children where they want to put a specific picture.

Variation

Although the artistic experience is diminished, the emphasis in group collages can be reversed. Instead of focusing on composition, the children can concentrate on cutting or tearing pieces of paper to decorate a large object. For example, the teacher can make a large cardboard pumpkin at Halloween and encourage the children to cover it with little scraps of orange crepe paper. During the winter, a giant cardboard snowman can be decorated with cotton balls or bits of construction paper. A large group can participate in this kind of project, and a strong feeling of group achievement may be produced.

This kind of collage may serve as a prop for storytelling or imaginative play. For example, a group of children could make three houses for playing out the story of the "Three Little Pigs." One cardboard box could be covered with paper bricks, another with twigs, and a third with straw.

The Bottom of the Sea

The Scene

A 3' x 5' sheet of paper is taped to the wall. Along the top edge of the paper is a line of blue waves. Scattered at the bottom of the paper are a few rock shapes. In the middle of the picture is a stick figure wearing a diving helmet with an air hose. Props include: crayons, small rocks and shells, dried weeds, and glue.

A Sample Script

"I want to show you a drawing I started," the teacher tells the children before free play begins. "This is the ocean. Well really, it's a picture of the bottom of the ocean down underneath the water." The teacher points to the water line on top and the rocks down below. "I'll just color some of these rocks," the teacher murmurs as she scribbles over them with a brown crayon.

"I think we need more rocks. Maybe someone can make some later. Anyway here is a diver. This is the diver's air hose. See the bubbles coming out of the diver's helmet? (the teacher quickly draws some bubbles)... Now, I want all of us to work together on this picture. Everybody can draw something. We need lots of things for the diver to look at...If you were under the ocean, what do you think you would see?"

As the children make suggestions, the teacher repeats them and prints them at the top of the paper. "Yes, that's good. We have sharks, whales, fish, eels, shells, octopus, ocean spiders, and crabs. My, you children know a lot about oceans. Well, whenever you feel like drawing on our ocean picture, take a few minutes and draw a fish or anything else. We need seaweed and flowers and rocks and sand—all kinds of things. I will leave the crayons right here by the picture. O.K., time for free play..."

Opportunities for Cooperation

Preschool children typically draw isolated objects or scribbles. By drawing a background scene, the teacher gives the children an opportunity to combine their individual artistic talents. The teacher in the above example chose an underwater scene because she knew the children were fascinated by the ocean. In addition, the ocean environment included many objects within the drawing capability of the children. Scribblers could make seaweed, rocks, coral, shells, and even fish. Children with more advanced drawing skill could make a whale, a shark, or an octopus.

The teacher anticipates that most of the contributors will come as individuals. The group drawing will attract children for a few moments when they are in between longer play episodes. Given a little encouragement by the teacher, they will add a fish or two and be on their way. A few children, those who are especially interested in drawing, will stay for an extended period of time. The teacher also plans to make an extra effort to invite shy or lonely children to the drawing, in an effort to get them more involved in class activities.

The teacher's role in this kind of activity is to encourage as many children as possible to participate. She makes no effort to draw a hard and fast line between adult art and child art. If a child asks for help in drawing a particular item, the teacher is there to give some pointers. On the other hand, she does not correct or critique the artwork of children who don't ask for help. The cooperation in this activity is most evident at the end of the project. The teacher shows the class what they have created. Trying to remember who drew which details, she congratulates the whole group for their joint accomplishment. If the theme has excited the children, and the final scene is sufficiently inspiring, the teacher tells a story based on the picture. So far the teacher has tried the following themes:

The sky

A haunted house

The bottom of the ocean

"Maybe next time," she decides, "I will try a flower garden. I can draw clusters of stems with leaves, and the children can draw the flowers."

Preschool children typically draw isolated objects or scribbles. By drawing a background scene, the teacher gives the children an opportunity to combine their individual artistic talents.

The Long Painting

The Scene

A chain link fence is lined with brown wrapping paper. Props include: cans filled with different colors of water-based paint and easel brushes.

A Sample Script

The teacher asks some children to help her unroll the paper and attach it to the fence with clothespins. "I need a city," she shouts to everyone within hearing range. Placing a can of green paint on the ground in front of the paper, she continues, "This is the green section." In short order, a red section, a black section, and a purple section are defined in the same way. The children who begin to paint seem to understand what the teacher means. The cans of paint are left in place while the children change colors and brushes by moving from spot to spot along the mural.

"Draw me a city at night," the teacher tells the children. "What do you see at night? What comes out at night? What are you afraid of at night?" With each question the teacher's voice is more dramatic, and a playful lilt becomes more pronounced. Monster blobs—some with eyes, others with horns or teeth—appear on the paper. Moons in several colors shine down on them. There are bugs, lightning bolts, rainstorms, clouds, fire, police cars, and darkness—indeterminate shapes and shadows everywhere. Scattered throughout this alien landscape are a few brave figures and an occasional house or light pole.

The teacher passes up and down the line of painters, talking for a few moments with each one, calling the attention of the group to an interesting new idea. "As soon as this dries," she says, "we'll hang it in the classroom."

"Can we work on it tomorrow?" one of the children asks. "You bet," the teacher answers, "I have some nighttime magazine pictures we can use."

Opportunities for Cooperation

In this example, the enthusiasm of the teacher is infectious. Children are painting with greater intensity than usual. Nevertheless, it is clear that this is not the first time the class has undertaken such a project. In the beginning, the teacher simply put the paint out and let the children cover the paper with designs. Later the idea of a city was introduced. The teacher announced that she wanted houses in one section, flowers in another, rocket ships in another, etc. (Her notion of a city was flexible.) Although the children paid only partial attention to the teacher's cheerful bossiness, the whole painting began to assume a recognizable character.

Another technique the teacher has used to keep the children concentrating on a painting is to work on it over several days. The first day the children paint, the next day they may draw, the next day they may paste real objects (leaves, buttons, seeds, etc.) on the picture, and the next day they may paste magazine pictures on it. Over time, the children have come to realize that the teacher will help them organize a group painting and that the final product will be unique and complex. It will be their own special creation to look at, touch, and talk about.

COOKING

Organizing Ideas

With her hand in an oversized oven mitt, Rachel pulled an empty pan from the playhouse oven. She scooped a make believe brownie onto a small tin plate and handed it carefully to the classroom visitor. "No, no! Don't eat it yet," she warned. "It's too hot. I gotta blow it for you first." After several exaggerated puffs, Rachel pronounced the brownies just right for eating. Obediently the classroom visitor tasted the brownies, and assured Rachel that they were the best she had ever eaten.

Children at a very early age recognize the special significance of preparing and sharing food. Whether they are playing in the sand box, rolling dough, placing pegs in a board, or gathering together in a playhouse, pretending to make and serve food is a favorite theme. Food is a symbol of hospitality, and the sharing of food is an expression of mutual trust. Classroom activities that involve cooking and serving real food take advantage of the child's learned association of food with hospitality and celebration.

When a teacher structures cooking activities so that children work together, she provides a "double entry" to cooperation. As children divide the labor that goes into producing a favorite dish, they have a chance to discover the tangible benefits that come from working together. When the cooking is over and the eating begins, children once again savor the fruits of cooperation. Passing a treat around the classroom, serving a special guest, or carrying a napkin full of crushed cookies home to the family provide an opportunity to enjoy the experience of sharing.

Another benefit of cooking is the opportunity to cooperate across generations. The child who has learned a few cooking steps at school is much more likely to cook at home with parents or relatives. Grandparents, who often cook more leisurely than parents, will especially treasure the help that preschool children offer.

A final advantage of cooking is the opportunity it provides for cross-cultural sharing. When parents from different ethnic backgrounds are invited to be cooking tutors or "chefs of the week," children learn to appreciate individual differences. Shaping a pizza, twisting challa bread, or eating rice with a pair of chop sticks—these are the happy experiences that children never forget.

Children at a very early age recognize the special significance of preparing and sharing food. Whether they are playing in the sand box, rolling dough, placing pegs in a board, or gathering together in a playhouse, pretending to make and serve food is a favorite theme.

Although most teachers would agree that cooking is a valuable experience, very little cooking takes place in preschool classrooms. As one teacher put it, "It's just too much of a hassle." Cooking projects require time, energy, and money. Certainly there is justification in these objections, but teachers who institute cooking as a routine activity find ways to circumvent them. Here is a list of helpful hints from some pros in classroom cooking:

1. Invest in a preschool recipe book, such as *Creative Food Experiences for Children*, by Mary T. Goodwin and Gerry Pollen.

2. Plan cooking activities that can be done in shifts, so that everyone gets a chance to participate.

3. Choose simple recipes for children's first introduction to cooking—like a milkshake made in a blender, pop corn, or instant pudding.

4. Develop a pictograph board for your recipes. Pictograph boards can be made in two ways. The first way is to use a large poster board or flip chart and describe the steps of the recipe with a combination of words, pictures, and symbols. Start on the top of the sheet with the ingredients and then list each of the steps. A second way to do a pictograph is to describe each step of the recipe on a sheet of paper and put up the papers on a wall or bulletin board in a left-to-right order. The second system takes a little longer to do, but provides an opportunity to use more pictures and more words for each step. Also, once you have completed the recipe, it may be easier to store a stack of papers than a poster board.

5. Whatever type of pictograph you use, be consistent in the selection of symbols. For example, an oven mitt can symbolize "heat up" and a red dot can stand for "this is the step the teacher does."

6. Make the clean up as exciting as the cooking. You can use badges, aprons, or chef hats to designate "washers," "dryers," "table wipers," "sweepers," and "put awayers."

On the following pages, three examples of cooperative cooking in the classroom are described. The point of these examples is not to suggest specific recipes, but to give general strategies for organizing classroom cooking. The first example involves a typical sequential recipe, in which ingredients must be poured, chopped, and mixed in the proper order. This is the most difficult kind of recipe to use in classroom cooking because some children are likely to grow restless, while other children are performing their appointed tasks. One way to reduce this problem is to organize the work according to teams. Each step will then go faster, and more than one child can be working at a time. If teamwork is not practical, try to find roles for the children who are watching. For example, as one child mixes the batter, the other children can watch for changes in consistency or count the number of strokes.

Sometimes a sequential recipe can be organized in terms of an assembly line, as shown in the second example. It is not always a simple matter to

Cooking projects require time, energy, and money. Certainly there is justification in these objections, but teachers who institute cooking as a routine activity find ways to circumvent them.

get everyone assigned to the right job, but once the assembly line starts, each child has a continuous job. Everyone is involved all the time.

The third example presents another way to involve everyone simultaneously. The children each prepare their own product, but they cooperate by sharing a common collection of ingredients. This parallel form of cooking is the simplest kind of cooperative cooking. The cooperation consists of imitation and friendly conversation.

No matter how much preplanning is done, adult supervision is a necessity in classroom cooking. But this also means that children get to participate with grownups in making a genuine product. Pride, laughter, excitement, delight; these are the emotions that children and adults share as they cook together.

Cooking Partners (an example of sequential cooking)

The Scene

A low table is set up in the art or science area. A portable oven has been placed on a side board out of the reach of children. Props include: two mixing bowls, a rolling pin and two pie pans, a small measuring cup, several spoons and knives, Bisquick, a squeeze bottle of liquid butter, raisins, dates, and chopped nuts in separate bowls, a jar of marmalade, and a timer.

A Sample Script

The children and teacher are grouped informally around the table. "Who can remember what we're going to make for snack today?" the teacher asks, directing the attention of the children to the task at hand.

Dennis:	I know, trucks.
Patricia:	Not trucks. Dump trucks, silly.
Teacher:	That's right, we're making a special kind of pie called a dump truck pie. Turning to the wall behind her, the teacher points to a pictograph recipe: "O.K. chefs, we better get to work. Let's look at the recipe. Here's our first picture. It's a picture of an oven.
Chorus:	Turn on the oven. (Teacher turns on the portable oven.)
Teacher:	Now let's look at our second picture. What do we see? ... Two packages of Bisquick, one small cup of butter, and four spoons of water.
Jeff:	I want to be the mixer.

No matter how much preplanning is done, adult supervision is a necessity in classroom cooking. But this also means that children get to participate with grownups in making a genuine product. Pride, laughter, excitement, delight; these are the emotions that children and adults share as they cook together.

Teacher: That's right—we need to mix those things together. Let's have a mixing team. Jeff, you and Amy open the two Bisquick packages and pour them into the bowl...And Jonathan, you measure a small cup of butter and pour it in... Now, I will add four spoons of water.
(The mixing team takes turns mixing.)

Chorus: What do we do?

Teacher: We have to look at picture number 3. Oh yes, raisins, dates, nuts, and marmalade. We need a chopping team. Dennis, you and Valerie can chop the raisins, while Karl and Patricia chop the dates. Cut them into little pieces and put them in this bowl with the nuts. Be careful with your knives. .. I will add a few spoonfuls of marmalade.
(When the Bisquick is well mixed, and the fruit-nut-marmalade mixture finished, the children look at the next picture: dough, a rolling pin, and two pie pans.)

Teacher: Good, I found a job for me. Watch me roll out the dough for the bottom of the dump trucks. And now, line up everyone. It's time to dump the fruit into the dump trucks.
(Each child dumps a "shovel" full of fruit into the dump trucks, the teacher covers the fruit with a layer of dough and places the two pans in the oven. During the ten-minute cooking time the teacher reads the book *All Kinds of Trucks,* and leads the children in an improvised version of "The Wheels on the Bus.")

Amy: The timer went off. It's all cooked. I want the first piece.

Teacher: I'm glad you were a good listener. It's time to take our dump truck pies out of the oven. Everybody find a chair at one of the tables. .. Oh, are you good chefs! These dump truck pies smell delicious. One pie is for snack. And who knows what the other pie is for?

Chorus: For taking home to Mommy.
For taking home to Daddy.
For taking to Mommy and Daddy.

Teacher: For taking home to anyone you choose.

A sequential recipe, in which ingredients must be poured, chopped, and mixed in the proper order, is the most difficult kind of cooking to use in the classroom. Some children are likely to grow restless while other children are performing their appointed task.

Hoagie Hand-Down (an example of assembly line cooking)

The Scene

A low table is set up in the science or art area. There is a refrigerator or chest within easy reach. Props include: dull knives or craft sticks, and hoagie ingredients (lettuce, cheese, sliced tomatoes, ham, salami, mayonnaise, and sandwich bread).

A Sample Script

Handing out some aprons, the teacher announces, "O.K. cooks, you did a good job washing your hands. Now, put on your aprons. We're going to make an assembly line." The children look puzzled.

David: You said we got to make hoagies.

Teacher: Yes, that's right. We're going to make hoagie sandwiches. And the best way to make hoagies is to form an assembly line.

Stephanie: My sister got to go to assembly and...

Teacher: Right, Stephanie, but that's a different kind of assembly. When we make an assembly line, we sit in a row, and we all assemble—that means put together—the sandwich. Who knows what goes inside a hoagie sandwich?

Chorus: Ham, cheese, cucumbers, tomatoes, pickles, more ham, peanut butter, marshmallows.

Teacher: Oh dear, with all those things we'd have a very fat hoagie sandwich. Would you like to see what we're really going to use?
            (The teacher opens the refrigerator door and brings out six different boat trays of hoagie ingredients: lettuce, sliced tomatoes, ham, salami, cheese, and mayonnaise.)

Teacher: Time to get to work. Stephanie, you sit here beside me because you are in charge of lettuce. David, you're next with the tomatoes...

When six of the children have been assigned an ingredient, the teacher gives an empty tray to the seventh child, who is at the end of the row. "O.K., Cassandra," the teacher explains, "your job is to catch the hoagies as they come off the assembly line. Now here comes the first hoagie starting down the line."

In assembly line cooking, each child is assigned a job. Once the assembly line starts, everyone is involved.

Everything Sandwiches (an example of simultaneous cooking)

The Scene

A low table is set up in the science or art area. Props include: cutting boards and knives, a mixing bowl and several spoons, bananas, tangerines, bread, and a jar of peanut butter.

A Sample Script

"Can anyone guess what kind of sandwich we are serving for snack today?" the teacher asks with a mischievous grin.

Chorus: Peanut butter...Banana...Marmalade... Koolaid...Poolade...

Teacher: My goodness, I think we're getting silly. But that's all right. We're making a silly kind of sandwich today. It's called an everything sandwich.

Pam: Yeh, that's silly. What's an everything sandwich?

Teacher: An everything sandwich is when each of you gets a piece of bread and you put everything on it you want. First, of course, we have to get the "everything" part ready. Connie and José, how would you like to slice the bananas? Savannah and Allison, you can stir the peanut butter until it gets nice and soft. And Pam and Arturo, I bet you can do a fine job peeling the tangerines.

(When all the ingredients are prepared, they are placed in the center of the table. Then the children are given slices of bread, and they choose their own ingredients.)

Connie: I only like peanut butter.

Teacher: You mean you're going to eat an "only thing" sandwich instead of an everything sandwich?

José: I like everything. See I'm making a big stack of bananas on my sandwich.

Teacher: Yes, you'd better eat your everything sandwich before everything falls on the floor.

Simultaneous cooking is the simplest kind of cooking. Children make their own product but they cooperate by sharing a common collection of ingredients.

CIRCLE TIME ACTIVITIES

Organizing Ideas

Circle times in most preschool settings are routine daily activities. The early morning circle time gives the teacher an opportunity to discuss the day with the children and to help children plan their activities. The afternoon circle time gives the teacher and the children an opportunity to review the day and talk about its highlights. These routine circle times also serve as transition from home to school and vice versa and provide children with a sense of identity and cohesiveness.

When children arrive at circle time in the morning, they are brimming with good news about things that have happened at home. There is an understandable tendency in such situations for preschool children to relate individually to the teacher. Each child's story is likely to mean more to the teacher than to the other children. And the children naturally expect the teacher to take the lead in planning and summarizing. Routine circle activities, however, can also set the stage for cooperative play by giving the children an opportunity to become better acquainted. Having gathered together to converse about school and home, the children rub shoulders with peers whom they may not play with the rest of the day. The teacher can develop routines that encourage the children to make brief, friendly contact with one another, such as holding hands in a circle game, see-sawing with a partner, or marching in a circle, with each child placing his hands on the shoulders of the child in front of him.

When children join the afternoon circle time, they are usually ready to wind down. In addition to reviewing the highlights of the day, teachers are likely to use this time for reading stories, listening to records, and talking about the next day. Teachers also use this time to give children take-home messages.

In addition to the morning and afternoon circle times, most teachers gather the children together as a group at least once or twice during the day. In some classrooms these midday groups are built into a daily schedule. In other classrooms they are called together spontaneously, as needs or opportunities arise. These midday meetings provide teachers with opportunities to introduce cooperative games, class projects, or theme-related cooperative activities.

Routine circle times serve as transition from home to school and vice versa and provide children with a sense of identity and cohesiveness.

The suggestions in this chapter are divided into three categories—opening circle, midday circle, and afternoon circle suggestions. Naturally, it is up to each classroom teacher to determine which suggestions to select and when to introduce them.

MORNING CIRCLE ACTIVITIES
Shake Hands with a Friend

The Scene

A poster board is set up on an accessible wall in the classroom with several rows of hooks. Props include: individual photographs of the children that can be hung from the hooks.

A Sample Script

As the children enter the classroom, a teacher aide helps them find their pictures on the poster and turn them face down. When all the children have arrived, the teacher gathers the children around the poster and directs their attention to the photographs. "Let's see who is not here today. I see Terry's picture, so Terry must be missing. Does anyone see Terry? No? Well, maybe she's sick. I see Brett's picture. Is he missing too? Oh, there you are Brett. I guess you forgot to turn your picture over."

The group continues to consider the pictures of missing children. Then the teacher switches to a guessing game. "Now let's try to guess who's behind some of these pictures. Let's see, how about this one? I wonder whose picture is under here. It's someone in this room whose name starts with S. She has brown eyes and brown skin and she is wearing red socks."

After four or five guesses, the teacher turns the photograph over. "Sarah," the class exclaims as a group. The teacher repeats the guessing game a few more times and then says, "Now let's sing our good morning song."

"Shake Hands With a Friend and Say Hello"

Hello everybody yes, indeed,
Yes, indeed, yes, indeed.
I said, hello everybody yes, indeed,
Yes, indeed my darling.

Shake hands with a friend and say hello,
Say hello, say hello.
I said shake hands with a friend and say hello,
Yes indeed my darling.

Most of the children shake hands shyly with a few neighbors, although a couple of boisterous characters circulate through the whole class, imitating the glad handshake of the teacher. The group settles itself once again, and the teacher describes some activities that she has set up in the interest centers. "You can choose any center you want, as long as there is room, but just remember," she tells them as they prepare to break up, "if you are through playing with something, put it back on the shelf. And when you hear the clean-up record, it is time to stop playing and start cleaning up."

Opportunities for Cooperation

This example is taken from a day at the beginning of the school year. The teacher is using the photograph activity to help the children learn each other's names, and the good morning circle also includes a review of important classroom rules, such as the procedure for cleaning up. As the children become familiar with their classmates and the rules of the classroom, the good morning circle will no longer be devoted to such topics. The teacher may simply ask the children to look around them and help figure out who is missing.

Shaking hands with a friend, however, will remain a central ingredient in the good morning circle. The teacher will keep introducing new ways to begin the day by giving a friend a special greeting. One day the children may try "gimme a game of five" or "high five," in the manner of athletes. Another day the teacher will ask the children to touch each other with just one finger. Perhaps she will ask them to shake hands with their left hand or to use both hands simultaneously. Maybe the teacher will show them how a group of children can stack their hands in a pile. From time to time the teacher will suggest that the children pair off and dance ("Round and Round and Round We Go"), then change partners and dance again.

As the children become familiar with the classroom, good morning circle time can be devoted to a variety of topics.

Show and Share

The Scene

The class has been divided into two groups. Each group is sitting in a circle with an adult. Behind each adult is a low table.

A Sample Script

"O.K. children," the teacher begins, "let's be quiet. Today is Friday and, as you know, every Friday we have 'Show and Share.' Who brought something from home to show?"

"Me, teacher," a girl yells triumphantly. "Me too, me too" several other voices chime in. The teacher calls on the first girl, who shows a seashell she got on a recent vacation to Hawaii. "You can hear the ocean in it," she informs the other children. "Thank you, Sabrina," the teacher says. "That's a beautiful shell, please put it on the 'Show and Share' table and then it will be someone else's turn." Gradually the table fills up as other children show their prize possessions: a toy race car, a coin purse full of marbles, a paper-weight that makes a snowy scene when turned upside down, an action figure, etc. The teacher explains to the children that there will be a ten-minute sharing period. During this period, the items must remain on the table, but anyone can play with them. The teacher reminds the children that the objects on the table are special things, which need to be handled with care. "If you don't want to play at this Show and Share table," the teacher concludes, "you can go see what is on the other Show and Share table or find something quiet to do in the classroom."

Opportunities for Cooperation

Frequently, the traditional practice of "Show and Tell" does not succeed in promoting interaction between children. The child who is showing something directs his remarks to the teacher, while the other children gaze around the room and squirm restlessly. Their natural inclination is to handle and play with the object that is shown to them, and they are unable to sustain interest when limited to admiring something from afar. "Show and Share" is a logical extension of "Show and Tell." The children are encouraged to bring items from home that they are willing to let other children touch, at least during a limited period of close supervision. The process of showing possessions from home becomes directed more toward peers and less toward the teacher.

Show and Share is most successful when conducted in a medium-sized group. If the group is too small, children don't have enough opportunity to listen to each other. If the group is too large, the children may get restless as they wait for their turn. It is the sharing period that really appeals to the children, and a medium-sized group produces a favorable ratio between

"Show and Share" is a logical extension of "Show and Tell." The children are encouraged to bring items from home that they are willing to let other children touch, at least during a limited period of close supervision.

showing and sharing. It also allows the teacher to relax rules of courtesy. In the previous example, the teacher simply asked who wanted to show something, knowing full well that several children would shout at once. The teacher chose this approach, as opposed to going around the circle and asking each child in turn, because informality encourages greater involvement on the part of the children. Informality also breeds boisterous interjections and arguments, but such disruptions are manageable in a group of 8-10 children.

Show and Share provides an excellent opportunity for teachers to model generosity and trust. From time to time they can bring some of their own possessions and let the children handle them. By sharing something of her own from home, the teacher can model the kind of objects that are appropriate for "Show and Share"—things that are special but, at the same time, not so fragile or valuable that they cannot be handled by a group.

MIDDAY CIRCLE ACTIVITIES

A Treasure Hunt

The Scene

The whole class is seated in a circle, anticipating snack time.

A Sample Script

"Today," the teacher begins, "we're going to have a treasure hunt, and the treasure will be our snack." Handing out a Zip-Lock bag to each child, the teacher continues, "Here is your treasure chest." Then she gives the children the treasure—peanut butter and cracker sandwiches wrapped in wax paper. After the children have put the crackers in their bags and zipped them up, the teacher and her aide collect the treasure chests. "I'm going to hide these out on the playground," the teacher says, "and then we will have the treasure hunt." While she is gone the aide explains the rules of the hunt. Each person can find as many treasures as possible, but can keep only one.

Having been told by the teacher that they may begin, the children race onto the playground and frantically search for the cracker sandwiches. Whenever a child finds a second or third treasure, a nearby adult gently suggests that the treasure be shared with a friend who does not have any.

A few children, who seem unusually empathetic, go so far as to help others look for a treasure. In a matter of minutes the hunt is over, and the children enjoy a communal feast under the tree on the playground.

Opportunities for Cooperation

The stage is set for sharing in this activity by limiting the treasure to one per child. The children are made aware of this fact before the hunt begins, and therefore they recognize that it is unfair for anyone to have more than one treasure. In this example, the one-to-one correspondence between children and treasure was established by having the children prepare treasure chests. An alternative, which promotes counting skills, is to let the children count the total number of children in the group and then count out an equal number of treasures. Treasures can be snack items, pennies, balloons, shells, pine cones, or any inexpensive item that is appropriate to give to the children.

Having built a foundation for cooperative treasure hunting, it is surprising how readily the children will share. Individual competition still whets the appetite of the hunters, for each child can find more than one treasure. But as children give away the extra treasures, they find their feeling of individual accomplishment is associated with generosity rather than accumulation. Skill in finding treasure is used to help others, not to build up the self at the expense of others. Of course, teachers will want to have a few extra treasures on hand, in case some cannot be found or are secretly confiscated. In general, however, this kind of treasure hunt combines high excitement with enthusiastic cooperation.

Parachute Play

The Scene

A group of 6-12 children, sitting in a circle and holding a small parachute (10'-15' in diameter).

A Sample Script

"O.K. boys and girls, let's pretend we're at the ocean," the teacher begins. "Hold on real tight with both hands and shake the parachute." Ripples pass across the surface of the parachute as the children start the shaking. "See, we're making waves," the teacher says enthusiastically. "It looks like a flag, teacher," a child suggests. "Yes, like a flag in the wind," the teacher agrees.

Returning to her own idea, the teacher asks who wants to swim in the waves. One or two at a time the volunteers crawl onto the parachute and pretend to swim through the waves. "Try to squash a wave," the teacher calls out. "Sit on it, stomp on it, lie on it." The tempo of the swimmers accelerates. They hop up and down and roll across the parachute. But the wave makers double their efforts too, and the bubbles and billows continue unrepressed.

"Whoa," the teacher finally groans, "let's rest our shakers for a minute." The children stand up, and the teacher shows them how they can throw the parachute up in the air. As the children grasp the sides of the parachute, the teacher repeats her instructions, "O.K., now on three, everybody lift the parachute up and let go...One, two, three." Several tries later, the group succeeds in floating the parachute above their heads. "Now the parachute is a cloud," the teacher explains. "Who wants to run inside the cloud?"

The next time the parachute is released, those who feel brave enough huddle together in the middle of the circle. The cloud descends on them, and they are trapped in a silken fog. Screams of pleasure issue from the collapsed parachute. "Help them get out," the teacher tells the group outside the parachute, and in a moment the fog lifts. "Let's do that again," a cloud explorer huffs and puffs as he emerges from the tangle of bodies inside the circle.

Opportunities for Cooperation

A parachute is a versatile piece of equipment, and curriculum guides often include a variety of parachute activities. Our feeling is that this kind of play is excellent as a special resource in a preschool classroom, but that the children are too young to coordinate and enjoy many of the possibilities. Group movements are best restricted to simple ones like shaking and lifting, and the activities are less fearful if limited to a moderate number of children using a small parachute. In order to suggest more ideas, we included both wave and cloud activities in our example, but in reality it probably would be better to try only one of these themes on a given day. Either one can generate at least 15 minutes of high-spirited cooperation.

As with any physical activity, preschool children participate readily when the play is given an imaginary dimension. Parachutes are more fun when swimming through ocean waves or walking inside a cloud. Another idea is to pretend that a parachute is a popcorn popper. Small rubber balls are placed in the middle of the parachute, and when the children shake it, the balls pop out in all directions. The cooperation in parachute play among preschool children does not come from building up complex play themes. It comes from the physical challenge of manipulating the parachute. The children have their hands full, quite literally, coordinating their movements.

As with any physical activity, preschool children participate readily when the play is given an imaginary dimension. Parachutes are more fun when swimming through ocean waves or walking inside a cloud.

Variation

Although young children need teacher direction to control a parachute's movement, they can use a parachute spontaneously for building. Rather than give them a parachute, the teacher may prefer to sew several old sheets together. When combined with chairs, low tables, or large cardboard boxes, this parachute substitute makes a fine cave, playhouse, tent, etc. A group of children can organize and maintain the construction with minimal help from adults.

Simon Says

A Sample Script

Divide the children into pairs. Explain that you will pretend to be Simon, and Simon will tell each pair how to touch each other:

> Simon says touch your hands together
> Simon says touch your feet together
> Simon says touch your bottoms together
> Simon says touch your knees together

There is no attempt to trick individuals by not saying, "Simon says."

Hot Potato

A Sample Script

Have the group sit in a circle. Each child spreads out his legs so that his feet touch the outspread feet of the children on either side. In this way there is no break in the circle. Place a medium-sized rubber ball in the middle of the circle and tell the children it is a hot potato, a poison mushroom, a stinky garbage can, or some other imaginary thing they do not want to touch. Explain what to do if the ball comes to them: "If the ball comes to you, push it away as fast as you can—don't pick it up—just push it away toward someone else."

Because the ball cannot escape from the circle (theoretically), the play of the children will result in a fast paced, cooperative game of catch.

With a little imagination, teachers can convert many traditional children's games into cooperative activities.

Upset the Fruit Basket

A Sample Script

A simple version of this game can be played with the help of two adults. The children sit in a circle, each child on a pillow or mat. While one adult leaves the room, the other explains the game: "I want to tell you a secret word—'pineapple.' That's a fruit. Now when Mrs. Bradley, the other adult, comes back, she is going to try to guess the secret word. We're not going to tell her, she has to guess it. When she does guess it, everybody jump up and yell 'yeah' and then run to another spot in the circle and sit down. Now let's try it once before Mrs. Bradley comes back..."

When the guessing begins for real, the adult in the circle can show the children how to give clues. The game can be played with a variety of categories, and eventually some of the children may want to play the part of the guesser. The high point of the game will remain the moment when the secret word is guessed and pandemonium breaks loose.

AFTERNOON CIRCLE ACTIVITIES

A Yoga Goodbye

The Scene

The children and teacher are sitting in a circle; it is time to go home. The teacher speaks to the children.

A Sample Script

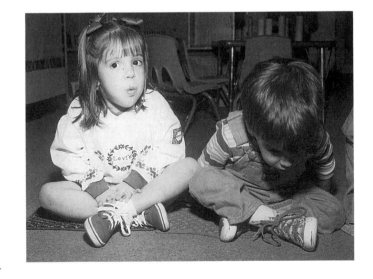

"Everyone get comfortable so you can sit nice and still. Put your hands in your lap. I want you to be by yourself for a minute...Close your eyes and listen to your heartbeat..Take a big breath and let it out slowly—like this—(teacher breathes in and exhales).

Now, pretend you are floating through the air like a cloud, and you are thinking about what happened at school today. What did you do that was fun? Don't say it out loud. Just think to yourself...Think about your friends at school today. Who did you say "hi" to?

Who did you sit next to at snack time?

Who did you play with outside on the playground?

Now open your eyes and look at your friends. Slowly, very slowly, lift your arms up in the air—stretch them way up high. Now stretch them out and touch your neighbors. Let's all sing:

> The more we get together, together, together,
> The more we get together, the happier we'll be.
> For your friends are my friends,
> And my friends are your friends,
> Oh, the more we get together, the happier we'll be.

(As the children and teacher sing, everyone in the circle sways back and forth.)

Opportunities for Cooperation

The teacher's goal in this activity is to help the children reflect on the friendship and cooperative play they have enjoyed during the school day. Naturally the reflection period is brief; the teacher does not expect extended meditation on the subject of cooperation. Neither does the teacher expect the children to engage in this kind of reflection everyday. On some days the teacher tells the children a summarizing story:

> Once upon a time there was a day called Wednesday. On this Wednesday, Bill, Paul, and Robin built a fire station. While they were building, Joan and Missy were playing with puzzles.

On the other days, the teacher encourages individual children to summarize the day by asking them questions:

> What was the best thing that happened today?
> Who did you play with today?
> What was your favorite toy today?

But whether the teacher chooses a silent period of reflection, a summary story or question-and-answer conversation, each day ends on a cooperative note as the children link arms and sing "The More We Get Together."

Magical Eyes

The Scene

The class has been divided into two groups. Each group is sitting in a circle with a teacher, and each teacher is holding a cigar box that has been covered with gold glitter and sequins.

A Sample Script

"This is a very magical box, girls and boys," the teacher in one group begins in almost a whisper. "Do you know what magical means? It means:

> Something that seems so true but just can't be...
> Something that might be true, someday a long time from now...
> Something that I wish were true, even if it isn't."

"Magical is wonderful," the teacher continues, "and in this box I have something that will make my eyes magical." The teacher demonstrates by taking out a pair of large rimmed glasses (with the lenses removed). The frame has been painted in garish colors. "When I put on these glasses," the teacher says soberly, "I can see all kinds of magical things." She stares at each of the children through the empty rims and chants:

> I see a tree...a tree with bottles of soda growing on it.
> I see snow...that is purple.
> I see butterflies...swimming at the bottom of the ocean.

The children sit transfixed. Although they doubt the words of the teacher, the illusionary power of the glasses has temporarily cast a magical spell over them. The teacher takes advantage of the moment and says quietly, "Now it is time for one of you to try the glasses. You will be the only person in the room who can see the things you tell us about."

The teacher taps a verbal child on the shoulder and ushers her to the front of the circle. "Put on the glasses," she instructs the girl, "and see the world with magical eyes."

"I see snow that is green," the girl begins. "And what else do you see?" the teacher gently prods. "I see," the girl responds, "a snowman, a green snowman—Mother Goose is making it."

"A green snowman," the teacher muses. "Yes, and the sky is purple," the girl says in a concluding tone. "What a magical scene," the teacher says to the children as she removes the glasses and puts them back in the box. "You know," she adds, "we don't want to wear out these special glasses. Tomorrow someone else will get a turn to put them on and tell us what they see."

Opportunities for Cooperation

The first few times this activity was tried, the teacher selected children whom she knew would be able to conjure up imaginary scenes. Having established the potency of the glasses, the teacher then made the activity voluntary. Only children who really wanted to look through the magical frames were asked to stand up in front of the group and describe what they saw. As the children became more comfortable with this pretense, the teacher encouraged questions from the audience. Following her lead, the children asked questions like:

> Do you see an animal?
> Do you see something to eat?
> Do you see something funny?

Naturally there were moments when the group was carried away with silliness, and all a child could see was "pooh-pooh" and "pee-pee." Then the teacher would simply announce that the glasses were getting worn out, and they went back in the box until another day. Occasionally, enthusiastic members of the audience also tried to compete with the child who was wearing the magical glasses. Although this competition was generally good natured, the teacher maintained order by reminding the children that only the child with the glasses had magical eyes.

After awhile the teacher added magical hearing aids (two cups cut from an egg carton and decorated outrageously). A child wearing these aids could hear animals and inanimate objects talking and singing. Then the teacher tried a pair of decorated boots. With these boots a child could walk anywhere. When children, bursting with fantasy, wanted to choose all three special items, they could entertain their peers by claiming to see, hear, and walk in the most unbelievable ways.

"Magical is wonderful," the teacher continues, "and in this box I have something that will make my eyes magical."

SINGING, DANCING, AND MUSIC MAKING

Organizing Ideas

This section covers three closely related activities: singing, dancing, and music making. All three involve self-expression through music, and all three are more enjoyable when performed in a group. Whether singing a song, dancing, or playing musical instruments, young children derive a special sense of excitement from group performances. The more successful a particular musical activity is in giving children this sense of excitement, the more likely it is to fan group spirit and build a cooperative feeling.

Although we think of music and dance as circle time activities, they can take place at different places in the classroom and at different times during the day. When children listen to music during finger painting, their fingers dance across the page and make delightful patterns. Playing a John Sousa record encourages children to keep time to the music as they march to lunch or out to the playground. And the very best way to get children to put away their toys is to sing a clean up song.

As we plan music and dance activities with children, it is important to remember that the process is more important than the product. It makes no difference if some children sing off key and some dance out of step. What is important is that all children participate and have a good time. Here are some suggestions for enhancing children's enjoyment of music and dance activities:

- Children enjoy songs that are simple and familiar. Songs that have a narrow range and repetitive chorus, like "Old MacDonald," "Twinkle Twinkle Little Star," or "Mary Had a Little Lamb," are perennial favorites.
- Give children opportunities to move freely in time with the music. Teaching children elaborate dance steps or routines can take the fun out of dancing.

Whether singing a song, dancing, or playing musical instruments, young children derive a special sense of excitement from group performances.

Records are available that are designed to bring out the creativity of teachers and children. On one side of the record are both words and music; on the other side, just the music. Having learned the tune and the general idea of a song, the teacher and children are free to make up their own verses as they listen to the background music.

- Rhythm bands can be very successful without expensive instruments. Children love to march to music shaking an orange juice can full of beans or beating out a rhythm on an oatmeal box.
- Children need opportunities to make up songs and improvise dance steps. Playing a waltz record and giving children silk scarves is a sure fire way to encourage creative dancing.
- Children enjoy music and dances from other countries. Parents who come from different countries can be an excellent resource.
- Select songs that can be sung in two languages, e.g. Frere Jacques, Are You Sleeping. Learning a song in a different language is a concrete way to extend a multicultural and anti-bias curriculum.
- Choose songs and dances that express a classroom theme. If the theme of the week is the Caribbean, you may want to introduce "There's a Brown Girl."

Back and Forth

A Sample Script

The teacher is working with two small groups. Group #1 is singing to Group #2:

> **Sung to the tune of "Frère Jacques"**
> We are lions.
> We are lions.
> ROAR, ROAR, ROAR,
> ROAR, ROAR, ROAR.
> Sing a song to us now.
> Sing a song to us now.
> What are you?
> What are you?

As the lions finish singing, the teacher huddles with Group #2. "What do you want to be?" she asks them. Apparently they decide to be chickens, for soon Group #2 is strutting around the room, flapping their wings and singing:

> We are chickens.
> We are chickens.
> CLUCK, CLUCK, CLUCK,
> CLUCK, CLUCK, CLUCK.
> Sing a song to us now.
> Sing a song to us now.
> What are you?
> What are you?

Group #1 responds by choosing to be dinosaurs. "What noises do dinosaurs make?" the teacher asks Group #1. They answer by growling and chomping their teeth. "Let's sing 'gobble, gobble, gobble' for dinosaurs," the teacher suggests. But when the group sings the song, a variety of ferocious noises continues to emanate from the hungry dinosaurs.

Opportunities for Cooperation

This technique is ideal for songs in which children can make up new verses, and each group is motivated to listen to the other. The teacher generally needs to take part in helping the children decide on a new verse. The teacher also ensures that each member of the group is aware of the decision, and she coordinates the performance by leading the song. A group may sing their verse a second time if the first effort collapses in confusion or hysteria. One group may be so pleased with another group's verse that they want to copy it. The mood is loose, and the rules flexible. The behavior of the children may grow increasingly boisterous, but by staying in control, the teacher can direct these high spirits into cooperative singing.

Variation

Instead of singing songs back and forth, two groups can dance back and forth. One group might dance with red streamers, one with blue. Or one group might be boys, the other girls. As dancing music is played on a record player, the teacher calls out the group to dance—first the red group, now the blue, now both red and blue together. The group that is sitting might also play musical instruments while they watch, such as tambourines or cowbells.

Serenading

A Sample Script

"Let's see who we serenade first," the teacher tells a small group of children. She is holding a plastic bowl that contains some slips of paper. At her invitation, one of the children reaches into the bowl and pulls out a slip. The teacher shows it to the group and announces, "The name is 'Jason.'" Continuing she says, "Today our serenade message is, 'You are nice.' The song goes like this:"

Sung to the tune of "Hello Everybody"
Your name is Jason, you are nice,
You are nice, you are nice.
I said your name is Jason, you are nice,
Yes indeed, my darling.

Instead of singing songs back and forth, two groups can dance back and forth. One group might dance with red streamers, one with blue. Or one group might be boys, the other girls.

Clearly this kind of singing is a common practice in the classroom. No sooner has the teacher finished than the children lustily repeat the song. Jason beams with pleased embarrassment. "Now, let's draw another name," the teacher says. "This time we will serenade...Jackie."

Opportunities for Cooperation

Certain songs can be adapted so that a group of children sings to one individual. This kind of communication represents a powerful form of cooperation. When it arises spontaneously, it often degenerates into a situation where a group of children taunts a peer. Under the supervision of the teacher, however, group communication to an individual can be kept on a positive plane. Singing a song gives the communication a simple, repetitive format. If the children grow bored with the message before all the children in the group have been serenaded, it is easy enough to create a new message. In the case of the example song, a variety of three or four syllable messages would be appropriate:

Your name is Jason, let's be friends.
... you're a boy.
... you're four years old.
... can you smile?

Variations

Instead of having the group serenade an individual, it is possible to reverse the procedure and encourage individuals to perform for the group. Most preschool children are too shy to enjoy singing for a group of peers, but they may perform a dance. The teacher can use a wooden box or low table to create an individualized stage. Then, when she plays a lively record, many of the children will respond to the beat and take turns dancing on the stage enthusiastically. Children who are reluctant to dance can still participate by climbing on the box and jumping off. The individualized stage focuses the attention of the group on the performer and reinforces the idea of taking turns. Although the level of cooperation between the performer and the audience will be minimal, this kind of activity helps children learn from each other and leads to more-complex group dancing.

Another possibility is to combine group singing with individual dancing. The group sings:

Did you ever see Jason,
Dance this way and that way,
Did you ever see Jason,
Dance this way and that way,
And this way and that way,
Did you ever see Jason,
Dance this way and that?

Certain songs can be adapted so that a group of children sings to one individual. This kind of communication represents a powerful form of cooperation.

Or more specific verbs can be substituted for "dance", e.g., jump, skip, run, etc.

A final suggestion is to introduce a song and dance routine where one child begins the dance and selects another child. In choosing the type of activity, be sure to take into consideration the age and language level of the children. With younger children, use only the first two stanzas and repeat them rather than introducing the whole song. Here are some examples:

The farmer in the dell,
The farmer in the dell,
Hi-ho and merry-o,
The farmer in the dell.
The farmer takes a wife,
The farmer takes a wife,
Hi-ho and merry-o,
The farmer takes a wife.

The wife takes the child...

The child take the nurse...

The nurse takes the dog...

The dog takes the cat...

The cat takes the rat...

The rat takes the cheese...

The cheese stands alone,
The cheese stands alone,
Hi-ho and merry-o,
The cheese stands alone.

(Children walk in a circle holding hands. The farmer selects one child to be his wife, the wife selects the child, etc. When the class sings "the cheese stands alone," everyone but the cheese returns to the circle.)

"There's a Brown Girl"

There's a brown girl in the ring,
Tra la la la la,
There's a brown girl in the ring,
Tra la la la la,
There's a brown girl in the ring,
Tra la la la la,
For she likes sugar and I like plums.
(One child stands in the circle while others dance around her.)

Then you show me your motion,
Tra la la la la,
Then you show me your motion,
Tra la la la la,
Then you show me your motion,
Tra la la la la,
For she likes sugar and I like plums.
(Child in circle does a motion, others imitate.)

Then you stand and face your partner,
Tra la la la la,
Then you stand and face your partner,
Tra la la la la,
Then you stand and face your partner,
Tra la la la la,
For she like sugar and I like plums.
(Child chooses a partner, stands in front of her, and bows or
curtsies.)

Then you skip across the ocean,
Tra la la la la,
Then you skip across the ocean,
Tra la la la la,
Then you skip across the ocean,
Tra la la la la,
For she like sugar and I like plums.
(Couple skip together around circle.)

Repeat song with new person chosen in the circle.

"Little Sally Water"
(All children stand in a circle, holding hands.)
Little Sally Water
Sprinkled in a saucer
(Children dance around Sally who is sitting in the middle.)
Rise Sally, rise!
And wipe your eyes.
(Sally rises and rubs her eyes.)
Turn to the east Sally
Turn to the west.
(Sally faces east, then west.)
Turn to the very one,
You love the best.
(Sally chooses a friend and stands before her and gives a hug.)

The person chosen then enters the ring and song is repeated.

New Verses

A Sample Script

"Today we're going to sing 'Mary had a Little Lamb,'" the teacher begins. "Except we're going to sing about our own pets instead of Mary's. Now, who has a pet at home?"

"I've got a dog, Teacher," pipes up a little girl in the front of the group. "Okay, good," the teacher responds. "What's your dog's name?"

"Rusty," answers the girl. "Did everyone hear that?" the teacher says to the group. "Melissa's dog is named Rusty...Tell us one thing about your dog, Melissa." Melissa giggles and says, "He licks my ears."

"Okay, boys and girls," the teacher announces, "here's how the song about Melissa and her dog will go:

Melissa had a little dog... "

Pausing for a moment, the teacher wonders, "Is Rusty really little, or is he big?" Finding out that Rusty is indeed big, the teacher starts again. She sings slowly.

Melissa has a great big dog,
Great big dog,
Great big dog.
Melissa has a great big dog
Who likes to lick her ears.

The teacher then encourages the group to sing the song with her. "Now, who else has a pet at home?" the teacher continues. "How about a cat?"

Opportunities for Cooperation

In order to combine creativity with cooperation, the teacher needs to select songs that permit new verses to be generated easily. "Mary Had a Little Lamb" is a simple song in which new verses can be created by inserting the name of the child, the kind of pet, and one statement about the pet. The teacher in our example could have made the verse about Melissa's dog even easier to sing by ending it with, "And his name is Rusty."

There are a limited number of songs that are appropriate for this activity, but here are three possibilities:

In order to combine creativity with cooperation, the teacher needs to select songs that permit new verses to be generated easily.

Sung to the tune of "The Bear Went Over the Mountain"
The Bear said, "Let's have a party,"
The Bear said, "Let's have a party,"
The Bear said, "Let's have a party,"
"And everyone bring food."
(The children think of an animal and a food)

The rabbit said, "I'll bring the pizza,"
The rabbit said, "I'll bring the pizza,"
The rabbit said, "I'll bring the pizza,"
"To eat at the party."

Sung to the tune of "If You're Happy and You Know It"
It you're happy and you know it, clap your hands.
If you're happy and you know it, clap your hands.
If you're happy and you know it,
Then your face will really show it.
If you're happy and you know it, clap your hands.

If you're happy and you know it, ride your bike (pantomime)...
If you're silly and you know it, make a face...
If you're itchy and you know it, scratch your nose...
If you're freezing and you know it, shake your head...

Sung to the tune of "Clap, Clap, Clap Your Hands"

Clap, clap, clap your hands,
Clap your hands together.
Clap, clap, clap your hands,
Clap your hands together.
Clap...Your...Hands

Tap, tap, tap your foot,
Tap your foot together.
Tap, tap, tap your foot,
Tap your foot together.
Tap...Your...Foot

Wiggle, wiggle, wiggle your nose,
Wiggle your nose together.
Wiggle, wiggle, wiggle your nose,
Wiggle your nose together.
Wiggle...Your...Nose

Variation

This approach to cooperative singing can also be used with records. Records are available that are designed to bring out the creativity of teachers and children. On one side of the record are both words and music; on the other side, just the music. Having learned the tune and the general idea of a song, the teacher and children are free to make up their own verses as they listen to the background music. Many of these songs, like the songs already suggested, involve singing and moving at the same time.

Being the Teacher

A Sample Script

The teacher is huddled with a group of four children. Quietly she says, "Now, are we ready? Remember how we start? Here's a green leaf, here's a green leaf." The teacher holds out her hands, palms up, as she speaks. All four children nod and smile. One of them says loudly, "That, you see, makes two."

"Shhh-not yet," another child warns fiercely. Getting up, the teacher leads the small group to a carpeted area, where the rest of the class is sitting. "Today," the teacher tells the class, "we are going to learn a new fingerplay. And here are the children who will be the teachers for today. Watch us very closely, and listen very carefully, while we show you. This fingerplay is called 'The Flower'." The teacher moves behind the four children to ensure that the class watches the child demonstrators. Then the teacher and the children recite the fingerplay in unison:

> Here's a green leaf, (extending one hand)
> And here's a green leaf; (extending the second hand)
> That, you see, makes two. (bringing hands together)
> Here is a bud (making fists)
> That makes a flower.
> Watch it bloom for you. (slowly opening fists)

After several repetitions, during which the child-teachers become increasingly exuberant, the whole class has learned the fingerplay. "Can I be a teacher?" one of the boys in the class asks. "Sure," the teacher replies. "The next time we learn a new fingerplay you can be one of the teachers. "Me too, me too," a chorus of children calls out. Smiling, the teacher promises that everybody will get a turn someday.

STORYTELLING

Organizing Ideas

Storytelling in a classroom requires and promotes cooperation. Children who are sitting together in a circle must cooperate with the teacher by listening and responding to the story. At the same time, they must cooperate with each other, listening courteously when other children make a comment and making sure that other children have a chance to see the picture. On a different level, story reading provides an opportunity to enhance cooperation. Books can be selected that sensitize children to the needs and feelings of other children; that focus on themes like sharing, helping, and working together; that celebrate cultural diversity; and that help children understand and cope with difficult situations.

One way to assure that children are active participants is to "read" the pictures in a book as well as the words. Young children love to talk about pictures and they often notice details that are missed by adults. The pictures may suggest a new variation for a story or introduce a new topic for discussion. Although preschool children are eager to hear the story that is written in the book, they also enjoy lingering over the pictures.

A second way to encourage questions and comments from children is to paraphrase a story. Many picture books are too long for a group setting. Paraphrasing shortens the story and enables children to get involved before their interest fades out. Paraphrasing also invites children to contribute because the teacher seems less oriented toward reading the words on a page and more oriented toward talking about the ideas in the story. The reading of the story takes on a conversational tone.

The third way to elicit cooperation is to find ways of letting children participate in the storytelling. Participation can involve taking a part, manipulating props, or acting as an echo or a chorus.

In general, the principal way to involve young children more intently in storytelling is to take the time to converse while reading; to take time before, after, and in between the events in a story. The children participate by relating real experiences in their lives and by fantasizing about imaginary ones. "Did you ever... What would you do if... Do you like to... How would you feel if...," these are the sorts of questions that bring children into

The principal way to involve young children more intently in storytelling is to take the time to converse while reading; to take time before, after, and in between the events in a story.

a group conversation and allow them to enter the province of the story-teller.

When children are very familiar with a story, or when a story is very simple, the cooperative dimension of storytelling can be extended still further. Under the direction of the teacher, the telling of a story can become a dramatic production, with children taking different parts. Sometimes several children can be the actors while the rest of the group is the audience. Other times all the children can be divided into two or three small groups, and each group assigned one character.

On the following pages, we describe some techniques for initiating conversation and organizing dramatic storytelling. These special techniques will not work with every story, and they would prove tiresome if attempted too often. In many cases cooperative storytelling is best served by simply reading, or paraphrasing, the story and talking about it. However, when used sparingly and in the right circumstances, unusual techniques can provide an added level of excitement to storytelling. The right circumstances occur when a story fits a particular technique and when you, as the storyteller, are enthusiastic about trying this technique. Pick and choose from the techniques we have suggested, using them as a springboard for developing your own storytelling style.

The Unfinished Story

The Scene

The reading corner is arranged so that ten to twelve children can sit in a semicircle around the teacher.

A Sample Script

Holding the book so that the children can see the pictures, the teacher reads the story:

> Jamaica climbed up the slide. There was a red sock hat on the ladder step. Jamaica took it for a ride. She slid down so fast that she fell in the sand and lay flat on her back. When she rolled over to get up, she saw a stuffed dog beside her. It was a cuddly gray dog, worn from hugging. All over it were faded food and grass stains. Its button nose must have fallen off. There was a round white spot in its place. Two black ears hung from its head.

"What do you suppose Jamaica is going to do with the dog?" the teacher asks. "I know," answers one child matter-of-factly. "She's going to leave it right there cause it's yucky." Timothy disagrees, "Bet she's going to take it on a slide ride."

"Well, let's find out," the teacher suggests, and continues to read the story. When the teacher gets to the part of the book where Jamaica takes the dog home, she queries the children again, "What will Jamaica's parents say when they see the stuffed gray dog?"

"I know," says the "matter-of-fact" little girl. "Her mama's going to say, 'Don't you bring that yucky thing into my house.' " Marianna has a different idea. "She's going to say, 'You bring that right back to the park cause it doesn't belong to you.'" After a few more children offer their ideas, the teacher goes on with the story. The children listen intently, curious to know what really happens next.

> Jamaica has returned the dog to the man in the park. She sees another child coming to the park. "Do you want to climb the jungle gym with me, Kristen?" Jamaica said. Kristen ran towards Jamaica, "Yes, but I have to find something first."

This time when the teacher asks the children to finish the story, several children respond with enthusiasm, "The dog belongs to Kristen."

"You are very good guessers," the teacher responds. "But how do you think Jamaica feels when Kristen keeps the gray dog?" A lively discussion ensues. One little girl, who has been very quiet up to this point, makes the final statement. "Jamaica is happy 'cause her friend's happy, and that's the end of the story."

The Story with Sound Effects

The Scene

The circle area has been set up so that 10 or more children can sit comfortably without interfering with each other's space. The prop is a story book that is interesting and full of action such as *Willis*, by James Marshall.

A Sample Script

The teacher holds up a new book and tells the group, "Today I want you to help me tell this story. Every time I start making funny sounds, you help me, okay?" Opening the book to the first picture, the teacher begins to paraphrase the story:

Once upon a time there was a very sad alligator named Willis. He cried all day because he didn't have any sunglasses for the beach. (The teacher and children make sobbing noises.)

His friend Bird felt sorry for him and said, "We will help you earn some money for sunglasses."

"Yes, we will help you." said his friend Snake. His friend Lobster just kept sleeping. (The group makes sleeping noises.)

Snake said, "sssssss," (The group makes hissing noises.) "I have a dime."

"Good," said Bird, "but we still need 19 cents more. Let's go find a job." Then the three friends got on Bird's bike and rode away. Lobster stayed behind because he was still asleep.

They came to a house and Bird said, "That house needs to be painted—that's a good job for us." All three friends started to paint the house. (The group makes painting movements and swish sounds.)

But look what they did. They painted orange spots all over the house. When the owner, a big hippo, came home, she was very angry. (The group makes angry noises and stamping movements.)

"I ought to step on all of you," the Hippo said. "Now get out. I won't pay you 19 cents."

Next, they met an elephant. He said, "I'll give you a job in my peanut factory. All you have to do is dip peanuts into candy syrup and make candy peanuts." After awhile Snake said, "Let's try eating some of these candy peanuts." The three friends ate more and more. (The group makes eating noises and movements.)

They felt sick. (The group makes groaning noises.) The elephant gave them some medicine, but he wouldn't give them 19 cents. "You're fired," he said.

The lobster woke up and said, "Let's have a talent show." The four friends built a stage for their show. (The group makes hammering noises and movements.) They told all their friends to come to the show. It cost one penny.

That night, at the show, the first trick was that Snake put Lobster to sleep. The way he did it was to hiss and move his head back and forth. (The group acts like a snake.) The second trick was that Bird played his cello, while Willis danced an alligator dance." (The group sings and dances.)

And do you know what? They made so much money that everyone got new sunglasses—even Lobster! He was asleep again. (The group makes sleeping noises.)

Reading or telling a story in which children contribute the sound effects elicits a higher degree of cooperative fun.

The Pseudo-Ventriloquist Story

The Scene

The teacher is holding a storybook that is interesting but hard for preschool children to understand, such as *George and Martha*, by James Marshall.

A Sample Script

The teacher asks one of the children to hold the book and turn the pages. "You see," says the teacher, "I need one hand for my friend, Judy."

"That's right," says Judy, who is a puppet. "I'm going to listen to the story too."

"This story is about pea soup," the teacher begins. "Yuk! I hate pea soup," mutters Judy. "Do you like it?" she asks the children. A chorus of "No's" confirms the fact that pea soup is not a preferred dish. "Well, that's interesting," continues the teacher. "Neither did George—this hippo here. He was over at his best friend's house—her name was Martha. Martha was cooking a big pot of pea soup. She gave a bowl to George and he thought he should be polite, so he ate it."

Judy speaks to the children again, "Maybe he liked the soup because his friend made it. What do you think?" The children seem a bit unsure. The teacher responds to Judy's comment. "It didn't make any difference for George, he still didn't like it. But Martha thought he did because he ate the whole bowl. She gave him another and George ate that one too. And then another and another and another. Finally, George had eaten 10 bowls of split pea soup."

"Why did he eat all that soup?" Judy asks the children. "Cause she gave it to him," someone replies. "Oh, I guess George didn't want to hurt Martha's feelings, did he?" Judy surmises. "Do you think he's going to throw up?"

"Of course not, silly," the teacher says to Judy. "But George was awfully full. Guess what he did when Martha gave him another bowl?"

"I don't know—what do you think?" Judy asks the audience. "Look," one of the children cries, "he put it in his shoes."

"That's right," says the teacher, "he poured the soup in his shoes. And he hoped that Martha wouldn't notice."

Judy stares at the children and wonders, "How is he going to walk home now?" Several ideas are suggested. Then the teacher finishes the story, explaining that Martha did see the pea soup in George's shoes and said, "Why didn't you tell me that you hated pea soup—friends should be honest with each other."

"Gee," George said. "Next time I'll tell you the way I really feel."

"Do you like cookies?" Martha asked. "Yes," George answered. And this time he really meant it. Martha brought George a big plateful of cookies, because George was still just a little hungry.

"Boy," Judy says to the children, "that hippo George can really eat, can't he?"

"Yea, he's gonna be fat," one child answers. "He already is fat," another points out. "Hippos are supposed to be fat," a third child states authoritatively. "Let's read another story about George and Martha," Judy suggests to the teacher.

The Puppet Prop Story

The Scene

A group of children is sitting around the teacher in a reading corner. Props include: tagboard story figures from a familiar story (in this case *The Little Red Hen*) glued onto craft sticks; a favorite book such as *The Little Red Hen*; and a plate of miniature rolls.

A Sample Script

The children went on a field trip to the supermarket in the beginning of the week. The man in the produce department had talked to the children about where the different foods they saw had been produced. During the week, the children had been especially interested in stories about farms. *The Little Red Hen* was particularly popular. "We're going to read *The Little Red Hen* a different way," the teacher begins. "I know, I know," Harold interrupts, "we're going to act out the story. I want to be the duck. I have a real good waddle."

"Well, you're almost right," the teacher continues, "We are not going to act out the story of *The Little Red Hen*, but we are going to tell the story with puppet props." The teacher lays out the puppet props in front of the class. Terence and Maria both want to have the pig puppets. "No problem at all," the teacher assures them. "We certainly have more than one pig on a farm." When all the children have selected a puppet, she begins the story, holding up the Little Red Hen puppet that she has reserved for herself.

"Will you help me plant the wheat, Mr. Cow?" The child who has the cow responds with gusto as he bounces the cow puppet up and down. "Not I, I'm busy, moo-moo-moo!"

Puppet props give children an opportunity to play out a story as it is being read.

"Will you help me plant the wheat, Mr. and Mrs. Pig?"

"Not I!" Terence and Maria respond in unison, punctuating their response with a loud chorus of oinks. The story continues at a fast pace until the Little Red Hen asked about who wants to help her eat the bread. When all the animal puppets volunteer to help, the teacher takes the liberty of changing the ending of the story by passing around a plate of miniature rolls. As the children pretend to feed their tagboard animals, or to eat the rolls themselves, a vigorous argument begins. "It was nice she shared, but she didn't have to," Veronica explains, " 'cause she did all the work."

"But it's not nice if you don't share," Bart insists, and the bread doesn't taste that good anyway."

Opportunities for Cooperation

Puppet prop stories encourage cooperation in several different ways. First, children have to take turns selecting a puppet. Second, children have to listen to the story carefully and respond with their puppet at the right moment. Finally, children have to give up center stage when their puppet has taken its turn. Inevitably, some children will require a little prompting both in taking and ending their turn, particularly if they're having fun making animal noises.

In choosing story variations to use with puppet props, try to find stories that are familiar and repetitive and that include enough parts. Animal stories are particularly good because animal puppets are easy to draw or trace and because making animal noises is both easy and fun. *The Three Little Pigs, Old MacDonald, The Three Billy Goats Gruff, A Fly Went By,* and *Are You My Mother?* can all be used with puppet props.

The Dictated Story

The Scene

The dictated story is a good activity for a follow-up to a field trip or a special event. Children are seated in a semicircle around a flip chart or large sheet of paper attached to the wall. Props include: a large sheet of paper or flip chart and Magic Markers.

A Sample Script

"Remember when we went to the farm on Monday?" the teacher asks a small group of children. "Today we're going to make up a true story about our trip. I'm going to write the story on this big sheet of paper, so we can read it when we're done." Pointing to some words at the top of the sheet, the teacher continues, "The tile of our story is 'Remember the Farm.' Ken, what do you remember about the farm?"

"That big tractor," Ken answers without further prompting. He is one of the least shy children in the class. The teacher prints on the sheet "Ken said, 'I remember that big tractor.' " The teacher encourages the children to start their statements with, "I remember" and she often asks them a follow-up question to help them elaborate their memories. Soon the following story has appeared:

Ken:	I remember that big tractor. I got to sit on it.
Stacey:	I remember the eggs in the nest. The chicken was sitting on them.
Chris:	I remember the horse. He ate an apple right out of my hand.
Mike:	I remember the school bus. I wish that I could drive it.
Jennifer:	I remember the stink. The pigs stinked the most.
Laura:	I remember the pigs—how cute. They nursed from their mother. And there were flies everywhere.

Having given each of the children a chance to dictate, the teacher reads the story to them. They talk some more about chickens and pigs. Later in the day, the group exchanges stories with another group. The stories about the farm are hung on the wall for several days and reread whenever children request them.

Variation

The teacher could have asked the children to remember the sequence of their trip to the farm: "What did we do first...what did we do next, etc." Or, she could have encouraged the children to begin each statement with, "I wish I were (something on the farm)." There are many different ways to proceed with group dictation, but it is easier to work together if the teacher gives the children a structure or framework for their ideas.

The Dramatic Story

In a dramatic story, the class acts out the story with each child playing a role. Once children understand the idea of a dramatic story, they enjoy acting out simple stories they make up themselves.

The Scene

A story that is interesting, simple in plot, and well known by the children, such as *Little Red Riding Hood.*

A Sample Script

Once every few weeks, the teacher puts on a special dress (actually it is her wedding dress) and becomes the storytelling lady. The children know that when the storytelling lady appears, the whole class will be involved in a dramatic production. Today, the teacher tells them, "The play is going to be *Little Red Riding Hood*"—a story the teacher has told the children several times recently.

"I need everybody's help," the storytelling lady announces. She asks for volunteers and soon has selected an announcer, actors, props (trees and houses), and an "ender." The rest of the children are the "clappers." They sit down in several rows of small chairs and wait for the curtain to rise.

The teacher positions the "trees" (four children) near each other and stations a house at either end of this pretend forest. Near one house are a bed, a blanket, and a pillow arranged on the floor. Each "tree" is holding a piece of paper with a simple drawing of a tree. Similarly, the children who are "houses" hold a piece of paper with a picture of a house. Little Red Riding Hood is given a hooded jacket, the wolf a furry jacket, the grandmother a nightcap, and the woodsman a cardboard ax.

The group of actors stands to one side while the teacher whispers something into the ear of the announcer. The teacher and the announcer then step to the middle of the imaginary stage. "This is the story of *Little Red Riding Hood*," the announcer tells the clappers. (Upon a signal from the teacher, they begin to clap.) As the applause dies down, the teacher begins the narration, keeping the story short and sweet. She adds a few details in order to give the props more of a role. For example, Little Red Riding Hood's house waves goodbye to her when she leaves for grandmother's; the trees sway as she walks through them; grandmother's house holds the wolf while the woodsman cuts off its head. Finally the "ender" comes to the center of the stage and holds up a poster with the words, "THE END."

Throughout this performance, the storyline has been interrupted by the clappers and by the teacher, who directs the stage actions. But no one is concerned about maintaining the illusion of a play. This is a production in which participation ranks higher than polish.

Variation

Once children understand the idea of a dramatic story, they enjoy acting out simple stories they make up themselves. The teacher can encourage children to dictate these stories during free play, and then they can be performed later during group time. The child who dictates the story also gets to pick the cast. As the teacher reads the story, the actors carry out the actions, and the rest of the class serves as the audience. A good theme for simple, dramatic stories is Superheroes. A typical story might be as follows:

> Wonderwoman chased a butterfly.
> Then she chased a bear.
> She danced around with the bear.
> They went to the park together.
> They had a lovely picnic.

A Suggested List of Authors

Any story can be used with the techniques we have described. However, teachers who stress cooperation will have a special interest in stories that focus on the feelings of children and their peer relationships. Here are some good authors who have written such stories for preschool children:

Varna Aardema	Barbara M. Joose
Margaret Wise Brown	Cherryl Kachenmeister
Jeannette Caines	Ezra Jack Keats
Nancy White Carlstrom	Anita Lobel
Lucille Clifton	James Marshall
Miriam Cohen	Bruce McMillan
Muriel Feelings	Ann Morris
Julia Fields	Robert Munsch
Taro Gomi	Mary Serfozo
Nigel Gray	Dr. Seuss
Eloise Greenfield	Judith Viorst
Virginia Grossman	Nicki Weiss
Barbara Shook Hazen	Charlotte Zolotow
Tana Hoban	

Teachers who stress cooperation will have a special interest in stories that focus on the feelings of children and their peer relationships.

THE PLAYGROUND

Organizing Ideas

A well-equipped preschool playground provides a variety of play materials. There are climbing structures for motor play, a sandbox, a playhouse, a variety of riding toys, and a grassy area set aside for ball play and other cooperative games. Although a playground can foster many different kinds of play, the focus in this section is on play that encourages sharing and turn taking, group interaction, friendship building, and development of pretend themes.

For the most part, outdoor play is characterized by a high level of peer interaction and a low level of adult involvement. Teachers generally do not take part. They supervise from a distance, stopping play that seems dangerous and settling serious fights. As time permits, they may help children learn new physical skills, or initiate a cooperative game that requires adult leadership.

Since the playground is seen by both teachers and children as a good environment for developing independence, playground equipment ought to be selected with this goal in mind. Obviously, the equipment needs to be safe enough to leave the children alone on, and it needs to present physical challenges that are neither too hard nor too easy for most of the children.

On a more subtle level, equipment can be selected that encourages peer interaction and sharing. For example, slides are usually better than swings for facilitating group interaction. Wagons invite more cooperative play than trikes do, although double trikes or trikes with a "back seat" encourage pairing up. Rectangular climbing structures, where children can climb across from or beside each other, are preferable to simpler climbing structures.

Playground equipment can be purchased that is specifically designed for cooperation, such as wheel vehicles built for two (or more), rocking toys that can be operated by a group of children, or slides that can be set up and dismantled by preschool children. One piece of cooperative playground equipment that is especially conducive to cooperation is a replica of a pick-up truck mounted on springs. A large group can stand in the back, and the more children who get on and jump up and down, the better the pretend ride becomes.

Playground equipment can be purchased that is specifically designed for cooperation, such as wheel vehicles built for two (or more), rocking toys that can be operated by a group of children, or slides that can be set up and dismantled by preschool children.

*Creating imaginary
play environments
on the playground
provides an excellent
opportunity to involve
parents and other
community members
in the school program.*

Playground equipment also gains cooperative potential when it is incorporated into imaginary play themes. Pretending naturally leads to peer group cooperation, and pretending on the playground is no exception. Wheel-toy play becomes more elaborate and includes more children when there is a gas station, a car wash, or parking meters and traffic signs. A playhouse can be supplemented with a fast-food restaurant and a telephone booth. An old rowboat or a tent can be added to the playground.

Creating imaginary play environments on the playground provides an excellent opportunity to involve parents and other community members in the school program. The adults will enjoy thinking of ways to turn the playground into a miniature town, and local businesses, including local outlets for large corporations, often times will donate equipment. Old parking meters and traffic signs can be collected from the city government. An oil company may donate a gas station sign and a display gas pump. The telephone company is a source of old telephone booths that can be cut down to child size. Perhaps McDonald's or Burger King will provide props for the fast food restaurant. Ingenuity and some hard work are required, but a beautiful playground for imaginary play can be built at minimum expense.

All of these considerations about playground equipment will make peer group cooperation easier, but they will not eliminate disputes. Often there still will be one too few trikes, one too many children wanting to operate the car wash, someone who is trying to monopolize a swing, etc. It is a fact of life that even on the best equipped playground some resources are scarce, and the only fair solution is to share them. Rather than shy away from this reality, teachers can view it as an opportunity to help children learn more about sharing. But first, teachers need to think out their own philosophy for sharing on the playground. When a child is steadfastly refusing to share a scarce resource, the teacher needs to step in and set clear limits. Even though young children are allowed to play more independently on the playground, they ought not to be allowed to bully or exploit one another.

SENSORY MOTOR PLAY

Although sand and water play work well inside the classroom, when the weather permits, there is no better place for sand and water play than on the playground. Sand and water facilitate cooperative play in several ways. First, sand and water are mellowing and encourage peaceful coexistence. Second, sand and water are plentiful and invite inclusive play. And third, as you will see from our examples, sand and water provide special opportunities for children to discover the benefit of working together.

Sand Soup

The Scene

The sand-soup script requires an outdoor sandbox and a nearby water source. Props include: one or two large kettles or 1/2 gallon pots, long wooden spoons, one or two soup cans, plastic soup spoons, a wagon, pails and shovels, and a short rope.

A Sample Script

Someone begins to fill a large kettle with sand and water. The teacher wonders out loud, "Are you making soup?" Throwing a handful of sand into the kettle, the teacher adds helpfully, "Here's some broccoli." After the kettle has been filled by several children, the teacher suggests that they put the soup in a "delivery wagon." The kettle is hauled around the playground and bowls of soup are ladled out for anyone brave enough to join the fun.

Opportunities for Cooperation

In this activity, too many cooks will not spoil the soup. As the kettle is being filled, there will be plenty of calls for "more sand" or "more water." Modeling by the teacher will quickly be picked up by the children. The filled kettle will be very heavy, and cooperation will be necessary to lift it onto the wagon. Maneuvering the wagon around the playground is more than a one-person job, too. By tying a short rope to the wagon handle, several children can pull the wagon at the same time. Most likely, there will not be many customers for the sand soup, but the group of cooks will enjoy pretending to eat it. The teacher might suggest they park the delivery wagon and have a picnic.

Variation

Instead of making a soup with lots of vegetables, stir up a witch's brew. Include frog legs, bat wings, shark teeth, or whatever horrible ingredients the children can think of.

Lakes

The Scene

The "Lakes" scene requires an outdoor sandbox, a water source, and a warm day. Props include: a collection of small boats, round cake pans (which are also used as boats), a wagon, several boards 4' long, and pails and shovels.

A Sample Script

One child is digging a hole and filling it with water. "Hey, I made a lake," he shouts. By now the water has sunk out of sight, but the child goes back for more. The idea catches on, and soon the landscape is dotted with lakes. The teacher wonders, "Shall we build a great big lake?" The teacher helps the children get started. "We need bulldozers and power shovels for this job," the teacher announces. As the shovels and pails scoop out the sand, everyone makes heavy machinery noises. Eventually it is decided that the hole is large enough, and everyone begins to haul water to the lake. Boats are launched. They bob around until sunk by sand bombs and giant waves, only to be salvaged and destroyed once more.

Opportunities for Cooperation

In the beginning, the teacher may need to initiate the group digging. A simple, "We need help with this lake," will draw several eager diggers. The cooperative effort of the group can be further solidified by piling the sand in a common receptacle—the wagon. Then the removal of this wagon and the dumping of the sand in another part of the sandbox become joint projects.

Older children may get interested in building a network of rivers or canals between lakes. It is difficult to keep the water moving in a sand channel because the water sinks out of sight so quickly. However, if a large enough group of water carriers is available, the excitement of forging a river bed may overcome frustration. Teachers also might experiment with lengths of gutter pipe, which the children could bury in the sand and use for rivers and canals.

Bringing water to a sandbox and pouring it into a hole is a splashy, squishy enterprise. And when the water begins to stay in the hole, the temptation to jump into this puddle is great indeed. Teachers need to anticipate that someone will get at least a little wet and muddy. A good way to divert attention away from wading in the water is to make a bridge across the lake. Providing boards of different lengths enables children to construct simple bridges for either human or toy vehicle traffic. Of course, the possibility of an accidental or intentional fall into the water still exists. There is no sure-fire method of keeping young children and water from mixing.

Buried Treasure

The Scene

Before the children arrive, the sand in the outdoor sandbox has been heaped into a mountain. A collection of painted stones has been buried under the mountain. Props include: one-dozen painted stones (gold, silver, copper, blue), four egg cartons painted to match the stones, and pails and shovels.

A Sample Script

As the children approach the sandbox, the teacher says, "I saw a leprechaun out here this morning. He told me there's buried treasure in this mountain—gold and silver jewels."

Immediately, three or four children start digging in the mountain. Cries of triumph accompany each discovery, "I'm rich...look at all my gold." Other children join the search, but they are too late to find much. "I'll share with you," a boy tells one of the latecomers. Another latecomer begs from the rich children, "Can I have just one piece? Please?"

"Let's put ours together," a girl proposes to her friend. "No one gets none of my jewels," warns another child. In the midst of this negotiation one of the miners turns to the teacher, "Is there any more?"

"I think you've found most of it. Let's put all the treasure in the egg cartons and see if any is missing. Look at these empty spaces," the teacher says, showing the children the egg carton. "There are two blue jewels and one piece of silver still buried in the sand. Keep digging."

Opportunities for Cooperation

In the beginning, this activity may be highly competitive; but after a while, the children realize that hoarding provides only momentary pleasure and begin to experiment with sharing arrangements.

The teacher can let the children pretend with the stones, asking them to keep their booty in the sandbox. Or the teacher can collect the stones and ask the group to help find the ones that are missing. A few children can help the teacher re-bury the whole collection. Once the children understand how the egg cartons are used to count the rocks, they may spontaneously organize additional treasure hunts.

Sandscape Gardening

The Scene

This scene requires an outdoor sandbox and a nearby lot with weeds that the children can pull. If the lot is outside the fenced-in playground area, an adult chaperone is needed to take the children on their plant collecting "expedition." If a free adult is not available, a collection of weeds and rocks can be gathered before the children arrive. Props include: several sprinkling cans, a wagon, small spades, weeds, and rocks.

A Sample Script

The teacher selects half a dozen children to accompany a parent volunteer on a plant-gathering mission. Pulling the wagon to a nearby vacant lot, the children dig up weeds that appeal to them. Then they return to the sandbox and transplant their specimens. "Does anyone want to put a fir tree or a mountain rock in their garden?" the parent volunteer asks. Some children continue to decorate the weed garden, while others water the plants with sprinkling cans. The members of the plant-gathering group decide they need more greenery and so retrace their steps to the vacant lot.

Opportunities for Cooperation

Before starting to dig the weeds, the parent volunteer can explain that the plants will be shared, as the garden is for everyone. The parent also can encourage the children to work together in digging up larger weeds. Back at the sandbox, appropriate comments by the volunteer will heighten the group feeling:

"Here's a spot that still needs to be fixed up."
"Does anyone have an extra plant for Julie?"
"Shall we go dig more plants for our garden?"

Sandscape gardening provides a special opportunity to promote cooperation on the playground.

Water Painting

The Scene

A water table is set up close to a cement wall or part of a building. An outdoor table with supplies is set up close to the wall. Props include: several empty five-gallon paint cans, paint sticks, wide brushes, painting hats, and plastic squeeze bottles filled with water of different colors.

A Sample Script

As two boys approach the water table, the teacher points to the squeeze bottles and explains, "Here are some colors to make pretend paint, if you want to use them."

"I get red," exclaims one boy, grabbing the bottle with red water. "I want it too," whines the other boy. The teacher explains further, "The paint is for sharing. Let me show you. First I put some water into the paint can. Then I add a small amount of paint." The teacher squeezes out several tablespoons of blue water into the paint can. "Then I stir it around, and presto—I have blue paint." The boys work together making a can of red paint. They are joined by more children. Soon the colors are being mixed together, and eventually the paint is a shade of brown or black.

As some children continue to experiment with the colored water, other children haul the paint to a nearby wall and help paint it. The teacher stimulates this development by offering painting hats to the children and directing them to the wall. "Remember," the teacher reminds them, "we have to be careful not to spill paint on the floor."

"It's just water, teacher," a little girl points out. "Yes," the teacher agrees, "but we're pretending it's real paint, right?"

Opportunities for Cooperation

This activity naturally leads to parallel play. The children paint independently with their own brushes. Cooperation is most likely to take place in the process of making the paint. By providing very large paint cans, various bottles of colored water, and stirring sticks, the teacher encourages a higher level of interaction. Cooperation is also furthered by helping the children pick a painting project that is large enough to accommodate a group and yet small enough to be completed in 10-15 minutes. As long as diluted food coloring is used, the "paint" will not stain most objects, although it will temporarily darken them and give the children a sense of accomplishment.

Mud Dough

The Scene

A water table is set up on the playground. Props include: a wagon, several small buckets, small shovels, and child-sized baking pans.

A Sample Script

The teacher decides to change the water table into a mud table. A small group accompanies her to a good digging site, where they fill the wagon and buckets with dirt. The dirt is carried back to the classroom from the playground and dumped into the water table. The teacher adds a small amount of water, and the children begin to mix the dirt and water with their hands. A boy suddenly notices his hands and panics. "My hands are all dirty," he whines fearfully. "If they are too dirty, just wash them off in this bucket," the teacher reassures him. "Then you can play some more in the mud."

After about ten minutes of adding water and mixing it in, the children are satisfied with the mud they have made. The teacher now offers them some small pie pans and muffin tins. "Look, Teacher. I'm making mud balls," a girl happily cries out. Several other children like this idea and soon they are engaged in making bigger and bigger mud balls. "Where do you want to bake them?" the teacher asks. "You mean in the oven?" one of the children responds incredulously. "No," the teacher laughs, "usually we let the sun bake the mud—then it gets really hard. Where is a good sunny place, do you think?" After a short discussion it is agreed that a safe, warm spot for baking mud products is along the fence on the playground.

Opportunities for Cooperation

Mud dough, like Play-Doh, is used by preschool children for individual products. The material does not lend itself to joint projects, and the children's skills are not advanced enough for them to execute large scale sculptures. The greatest cooperation occurs when the children make the mud—when they dig and carry the dirt, and then mix water with it. Once the mud is mixed, most of their play will be imitative, but the process of transporting products to a baking spot will create additional opportunities for cooperation. Again, at the end of the activity, the children enjoy working together to clean the water table. Some of the children can scrape out excess mud, put it in a wagon, and haul it away, while others wash the water table with wet sponges.

Scrubbing and Polishing

The Scene

A water table or wading pool has been placed on the playground and half-filled with water and mild detergent. Props include: dishes and silverware, dolls with washable hair, plastic furniture, dress-up clothes, rocks, trikes, and wagons. Some appropriate tools for scrubbing include: scrub brushes, tooth brushes, washrags, squirt bottles, and washboards.

A Sample Script

"I thought our trikes could use a good wash," the teacher casually says. Pouring dish detergent into the water in the water table, she continues, "Stir this around and the water will have lots of soap bubbles." The teacher steps back as the children stir up the suds and then retrieve the equipment lying in the water— washrags, brushes of different kinds, squirt bottles, and tin cans. A boy douses one of the trikes with a canful of water. "That'll clean it up," he boasts. Other children approach the problem more deliberately. They use washrags to rub the trikes all over. One child discovers that the toothbrush is just right for cleaning in hard-to-get-to-places, like around the hubs of the wheels. The scrub brushes work nicely on the seat and the rear footboard.

Sensing that the children may be a bit disturbed by the soap bubbles that cling to the trikes, the teacher tells them they can get clean rinse water at a nearby faucet. The boy who earlier took such pleasure pouring water over the trikes is the first in line at the faucet. But he has plenty of help. Soon the trikes have been rinsed numerous times. "Let's clean 'em again," calls out the boy who specializes in dumping. This time he has a can full of soapy water. "Yea, more soap," the others agree.

Opportunities for Cooperation

There is a surprisingly large number of things in a classroom environment that can be washed. Even if the items are not terribly dirty, the children will enjoy the cleaning process. It is satisfying to slosh soapy water around, to see things turn shiny and glistening. In fact, young children are much more attuned to the sensual pleasures of scrubbing than to the quality of their work. If they are having a good time, they will wash something again and again. The cleaning becomes a playful ritual.

Despite its inherent attraction, this kind of cleaning is best if it ends on a meaningful note. The teacher may be able to help by suggesting a way to

Young children are much more attuned to the sensual pleasures of scrubbing than to the quality of their work. If they are having a good time, they will wash something again and again. The cleaning becomes a playful ritual.

finish the activity. Perhaps the trikes can be ridden in a pretend parade once they are clean. Dolls who have been washed can be dried and put to bed. Dress-up clothes can be hung on a clothesline.

Of course, the cooperation that takes place during these cleaning projects is not highly organized. Some children may choose to end their cleaning in a logical manner. Others will stop in the middle of the job. Still others will continue washing indefinitely. Each of these outcomes is perfectly acceptable. The goal of the activity is to encourage peer group interaction that is casual and relaxing.

Pass and Splash

The Scene

An empty wading pool has been placed in the middle of the circle. Props include: 10-20 small water-filled balloons in a bucket and a garden hose formed into a circle approximately 12' in diameter.

A Sample Script

Calling a group of ten children together, the teacher asks them to make a circle by standing next to the hose. This means that each child is about four feet from the edge of the wading pool. The teacher picks up a water balloon and cups it in both hands. "Do you know what this is?" the teacher begins as she walks around the circle, letting the children touch the balloon. "Feels funny, doesn't it, like jello."

"Like a water bed," one of the children adds.

Now the teacher announces that they are going to play a water balloon game:

> We are going to break the water balloons in the wading pool—wait, wait, everybody will get a turn. Richard (a boy on the other side of the circle) will go first. I will start this balloon around the circle. I'm passing it VERY, VERY carefully to Angela (the girl standing next to the teacher). Now Angela, you pass it to the next person.

When the balloon gets to Richard, he looks expectantly at the teacher. Is she really going to let him break it? The teacher explains that everyone will count to three and then say "splash."

"When we say 'splash,' " she says to Richard, "you throw the water balloon into the wading pool. A titter of excitement passes around the circle as Richard steps up to the wading pool. "One, two, three, SPLASH." Richard raises the balloon above his head with both hands and then flings

If the rules are followed by everyone, the result is a group feeling of excitement. All of the children feel they have taken part in the experience, and together they have been allowed to play with something that usually is off limits.

it toward the target. Drops of water fly in all directions, but the only person who really feels the spray is Richard, who beams proudly.

"Now it's Andy's turn," the teacher announces, picking up another water balloon and starting it around the circle.

Opportunities for Cooperation

In contrast to most water play, this activity is structured by the teacher. It has rules like a game, although there are no winners or losers. Like any rule-based game, cooperation lies in following the rules. The children cooperate by carefully passing the water balloons; they cooperate by counting to splashdown; most of all they cooperate by waiting for their turn. If the rules are followed by everyone, the result is a group feeling of excitement. All of the children feel they have taken part in the experience, and together they have been allowed to play with something that usually is off limits.

Variation

Another version of this activity, requiring special supervision, is dropping stones. A group of children standing on one side of the pool experiment with different dropping techniques, talking about the splashes and ripples, and noting the changed appearance of the stones when they are underwater. Using small rubber balls reduces the magnitude of the splashing and the danger of someone being injured by an errant toss, but it does not appreciably diminish the appeal of the activity.

PRETEND PLAY

Because the playground offers both the time and the place for pretending, the most elaborate development of a pretend theme is likely to occur during outdoor play time. At times, the play themes are active and exuberant; a band of pirates is planning a grand adventure, spacemen are taking off for a glorious moon ride, or a team of amateur athletes is practicing for the Olympics. At other times, the play themes are quiet and low keyed; a family group is packing up for a picnic, a self-appointed teacher is teaching an eager student how to count up to five.

Wheel Play

The Scene

A gas station has been set up in one section of the playground. It consists of a gas pump (wooden post) with a gas hose and an air hose, a variety of squirt bottles filled with water, a bucket of water with sponges and rags, and a toolbox containing a rubber hammer and screwdrivers. A convenience store is set up in a small playhouse with a long window opening out toward the track. Inside the playhouse is a paper-cup dispenser and a large thermos of drinking water. Props include: several trikes and wagons, rope, and a circular track that includes a gas station and a convenience store.

A Sample Script

With shouts of jubilation, the children burst out of the classroom door and run to the storage shed. It soon becomes apparent that the object of this race is to gain control of a trike or wagon. The school has a good sized collection, but after the teacher has distributed the vehicles, there still are several disappointed children. "Why don't you play in the gas station until it is your turn to ride a trike?" the teacher suggests. Her suggestion does not meet with universal approval, but two of the unhappy children do go to the gas station. "Who wants gas?" they yell out as the other children pass by. Gradually business picks up. Vehicles stop by and the gas station attendants pretend to fill them up with gas and air. "Wash my windshield," one driver says in a tone of self assurance. "Where's the windshield?" the attendant asks bluntly. The owner replies with a wave of the hand, "Oh, right there." The attendant slops water over the handlebars, fender, and seat. "How's that?" he asks. "Fine," the driver answers, sitting down on the wet seat and driving off.

Opportunities for Cooperation

In most preschools, trikes are a valuable and scarce resource, and the part of the playground where trikes are ridden becomes a high conflict area. A good way to decrease the frustration over not getting a trike is to provide some supplementary activities. A simple gas station along the path allows nonriders to participate in a different manner. The role of the teacher is to help all the children, both the riders and the gas station attendants, discover how the gas station makes trike riding more enjoyable. In the example, the driver whose seat got washed was not upset, but many times there will be trouble at the gas station. Possessiveness runs high among like operators, and their touchiness is contagious. Teachers often are needed to mediate disputes between those who have and those who do not have a trike.

Although a gas station is the most logical supplementary activity, another possibility is a playhouse structure that serves as a convenience store. The teacher can introduce the theme by installing water and drinking cups in the store and then offering riders a taste of their favorite pretend drinks. Children who wish to be storekeepers can take it from there, stocking the store with any kind of food treats or toys they can imagine.

Trike riding is strongly individualistic, even though two children occasionally ride the same trike. In general, children compete to get the trikes and then they compete while riding them. They tailgate each other, collide on purpose, and force each other off the path. These aggressive maneuvers are more acceptable when they are seen by the children as part of a race or game. A circular track encourages children to think in terms of a race. They get involved in seeing how fast they can circumnavigate the track and are less concerned about proving how tough they are.

The teacher also can soften the atmosphere of individual competition by offering wagons to the children. In contrast to trikes, wagons are more fun when used by two or three children. Making pieces of rope available can lead to even larger cooperative efforts. Several trikes may be hooked together, or a trike may pull a wagon.

In most preschools, trikes are a valuable and scarce resource, and the part of the playground where trikes are ridden becomes a high conflict area. A good way to decrease the frustration over not getting a trike is to provide some supplementary activities.

COOPERATIVE GAMES

Because most playground games require teacher direction, it is a good idea to reserve playground games for times when the group is small or when more than one teacher is on the playground. With a little ingenuity, almost any competitive playground game can be made cooperative. Chase games can be turned into rescue games, and races can become relays with children on one side and a stop watch on the other. The goal of a competitions can be to make the whole class the winner.

Races

A Sample Script

Divide the children into pairs and tell each couple that they are going to race by cooperating with each other. One possibility is a "don't spill the water" race. A bucket of water is suspended on a yard stick, and each child holds one end. The challenge is to carry the bucket across the playground without spilling any water. Another possibility is a wheelbarrow race, in which one child runs on his hands while his feet are held by the other child. The most direct way to organize a cooperative race is to have groups of two, three, or more children hold hands while they run. In fact, if the whole class holds hands, then the object of the "race" can be to complete the course without anyone letting go.

Follow the Leader

A Sample Script

Line the children up behind one of the leaders in the class. Explain that the leader will run through the playground and that everyone else must follow and copy. Encourage the leader to perform simple actions, such as walking along a balance beam or wooden plank, jumping off a low platform, crawling through a short tunnel, etc. After a few minutes, change leaders.

Hide and Seek

A Sample Script

Reverse the usual rules. Let one child hide while everyone else is "it". The "It" group closes their eyes and counts together to 20 or 30. Then they all look for the hiding child. Most likely, the children will search in several small groups rather than one large one, but there will be an element of cooperation.

Tag

A Sample Script

In the cooperative version of Tag, each child joins "it" when tagged. In other words, when the child who is "it" touches one other child, those two join hands and chase the rest. When either of them touches another child, that child joins and the threesome is "it." Play the game in a restricted space so that the group of "it" children can encircle children who have not been tagged. It also helps if the "it" children agree ahead of time whom they want to chase.

CELEBRATING FAMILIES

Organizing Ideas

"Parent empowerment" has become a favorite phrase among early childhood educators. The old idea that the appropriate place for parents in a classroom is planning parties and going on field trips is out of fashion. Teachers recognize that parents can play several different roles in the classes. They can provide important information and insights related to their own child. They can enrich the cultural diversity of the classroom by sharing stories and songs, artifacts, and traditions. They can bring their knowledge and talents to the children in the class. They can serve as educational partners by contributing ideas about curriculum and participating in policy decisions.

While full involvement of every parent is a goal to which teachers aspire, we cannot expect all parents to be active classroom participants. Some parents do not have time to devote to school activities. Other parents are too stressed or burned out to assume any kind of responsibility. There are also parents who have a genuine belief that home and school should be separated. Although it is certainly appropriate for classroom teachers to do everything they can do to encourage parent participation, it is never appropriate to demand it.

In this chapter, our focus is on finding creative ways of implementing a partnership with parents. In the first section, we look at ways of creating a family friendly classroom. Our focus is on ways of making the classrooms inviting to parents and soliciting their input. In the second section, we look at ways of expanding children's understanding of family. We suggest strategies for fostering a sense of family in the classroom and for introducing curriculum themes that focus on family values.

While full involvement of every parent is a goal to which teachers aspire, we cannot expect all parents to be active classroom participants.

SECTION I
THE FAMILY FRIENDLY CLASSROOM

While it is easy to give lip service to the concept of families as partners, unless we can make parents feel that they are welcome in the classroom and their contributions are valued, the partnership is only words. In this section, we describe two classrooms where the concern for family is salient. In the first classroom, the teacher has found a way of helping the children learn about each other's family. In the second classroom, the focus is placed on welcoming parent visits.

Knowing About Our Families - Classroom One

The Scene

One section of the classroom has been set aside as "The Family Place." The wall is covered with a large sheet of brown paper. Rows of single-family houses and apartments are outlined with a black Magic Marker. Family names are printed in large letters on the roof of each house or apartment. A nearby table is stocked with pipe cleaners, scraps of paper, yarn, crayons, Magic Markers, and glue or paste.

A Sample Script

A boy standing by the table holds up a twisted pipe cleaner, "I made a tree, see? It's to put on my house." The teacher brings over a small cup of glue. "Your tree looks great. How about finding the house with your name on it?" A second child interrupts, "I need glue too. My house needs a tree."

"Does not—you don't have a tree at your house," a third child insists. The teacher gives the second child a cup of glue. "Everybody in this class has their own house. Even if you don't have a tree at your house at home, it is okay to plant a tree at your pretend house." An enterprising child chimes in, "Well, I made a TV antenna for my house. And it's not going to ever get broken."

Opportunities for Cooperation

As the children continue to fix up their houses, glueing on pipe cleaner trees, telephone wire antennae, cotton snow, and tagboard people, one good idea leads to another. When the children begin to run out of ideas and space, the teacher introduces a new suggestion. "Why don't we build some roads between our houses so that we can visit each other. I brought in some brown yarn. Let's dip strands of yarn in the glue and join the houses together." Despite one child's insistence that nobody could come to his house, the idea of joining the houses with strands of yarn catches on quickly. Pretty soon the children create an elaborate web of yarn roads. At this point one of the children puts a large glob of paste on top of one of the houses. "It's raining, it's pouring, the old man is snoring." Before the rest of the group can follow suit the teacher announces "clean up time" and the activity ends for the day.

Variations

Creating a neighborhood works best in classrooms with plenty of wall space. Variations on the theme that take less space but are quite effective include family trees, a family treasure box, and family ties.

▼ **Family Trees**

Family trees provide children with a way of describing the different generations in the family—grandparents, parents, and children. A simple way of creating a family tree is to have children bring in photos of their family. Trees can be outlined on sheets of newsprint, and family pictures glued onto the tree. A simple tree would show grandparents as the roots, parents as the trunk and children as the branches.

▼ **Family Treasure Box**

Family treasure boxes provide children with the opportunity to bring something special from home into the classroom. Children may bring in something simple like the ticket stub from a circus that the family just attended, a special memento borrowed from a family member, dad's boy scout medal, grandma's paper fan, or perhaps a rock that mother found in the garden. In classrooms where different cultures are represented, children can be encouraged to bring in artifacts that reflect their cultures. Children are especially intrigued by tokens from far away places—a belt from Mexico, a paper crane from Japan, a necklace from Guatemala, a post card from Hawaii, a dreydl from Israel, a hazel nut from Brazil, etc. As children explore and discuss these treasures from different cultures and different countries, the strange becomes familiar, and differences in practice become a source of pride.

▼ Family Ties

Family ties is a simple weaving activity that can be achieved as a group project. A frame about 3' x 5' is constructed out of plywood with rows of twine strung from top to bottom. Each child is asked to bring a piece of cloth, a necktie or a scarf from home to weave into the hanging.

Welcoming Parents to the Class - Classroom Two

The Scene

The class is just getting started and a parent is standing by a bulletin board. The words "WE LOVE PARENTS" are written across the top of the board. One section of the board is labeled "Parent Swap Spot." Several notes have been tacked under it—For Sale: one crib—good shape. Wanted—to rent—apartment with 2 bedrooms. A second section of the board is devoted to notices—Kindergarten screenings on May 1st; Family Fair on Saturday, sponsored by Station WFNP; facts you need to know about HIV virus. A final section is devoted to "love notes" sent by children to their parents. A visiting parent is wearing a badge and ribbon with the words "Parent of the Day" written on it.

A Sample Script

The teacher begins, "Melissa would you like to introduce your father to the class?" Melissa smiles and shakes her head but doesn't say anything. A second child jumps up, "You're supposed to say, 'Class this is my Daddy—Daddy this is my class.'"

"Mr. Martin is Melissa's father," the teacher interjects. "He works for the telephone company and he knows all about how telephones work." Melissa's father takes out a small suitcase with two telephones, some wires and some small tools.

Melissa watches proudly as her father shows the children the different parts of the telephone. Finally, Melissa gets up the courage to join the conversation. "And Daddy climbs a telephone pole—real high—you should see."

Opportunities for Cooperation

Once a parent has accepted a classroom invitation to participate in Show and Tell, the parent becomes a classroom friend and advocate.

Once a parent has accepted a classroom invitation to participate in Show and Tell, the parent becomes a classroom friend and advocate.

Variations

Naturally, all parents cannot take a turn coming to the class. As a matter of fact, many parents are on such tight schedules that they cannot come to the classroom at all. When parents cannot come to the classroom, teachers need to find other ways of increasing communication.

▼ Send home biweekly notes or make periodic telephone calls describing interesting things a child did or said.

▼ Develop a class newspaper that includes pictures of participating fathers.

▼ Get a list of parents' birthdays and anniversaries and help the children in the class make a birthday card to bring home on special family occasions.

▼ Develop a class recipe book that includes recipes that have been contributed by the children's families.

▼ Plan a "Grandmother's Attic" day in which children share an artifact or memento lent to them by a grandparent—a scarf, button, tea caddy, sampler, medal, or family photo.

▼ Use parents as a resource to enrich a curriculum unit. For example, as an extension of the theme "It's a Small World," parents from different cultures and/or different countries could join show and tell at circle time or set up a culture-sharing display. As an extension of a "Working World" theme, parents could be invited into the classroom to talk about their job—or could serve as the sponsor of a work-place tour.

▼ Create a parent helper certificate so that parents who volunteer in the classroom are presented a certificate at the end of the day.

SECTION II
ALL ABOUT FAMILIES

In this section, we visit two classrooms where "The Family" has been selected as the theme of the month. In the first classroom, the focus is on the importance of families. In the second classroom, the family theme is expressed by creating a family spirit in the classroom.

Family Picture Sort - Classroom One

The Scene

Several children are gathered in the language area and are busily sorting through a basket of pictures. The pictures depict families from different parts of the world. All the pictures have been laminated and are fairly uniform in size. An assistant teacher has been watching the children for several minutes.

A Sample Script

"Those picture are fun to look at, aren't they?" the assistant teacher begins. "Would you like me to show you a really great game we can play with those pictures? It's called Family Dominoes. Sit around in a circle and I'll show you how to play it." The children, after a bit of jostling, sit around the assistant teacher in a circle. "Me first, me first," Jeremy shouts out. "Wait a minute," the assistant teacher interjects, "we can't start until I tell you the rules. First, I give you each four pictures." Each child is given four pictures. "Now I put one picture in the middle. Let's let Jeremy go first. Jeremy, look at the picture in the middle. Do you have a picture that is like it in some way?" Jeremy looks puzzled. "Maybe I can help you. Let's see. The picture in the middle is about a family eating dinner."

"I got an eating picture," Jeremy shouts, "but these children don't have clothes." Several children begin to giggle. The assistant teacher remarks casually, "That's right. The children in your picture are from Africa and they are not wearing clothes. What do you think they are eating?" Jeremy looks at the picture again. "I think it's fish. Do I put it next to the first picture?" "That's it. Frances, it's your turn to find a picture that matches." Frances looks troubled. "But I don't have an eating picture."

"You can still make a match," the assistant teacher assures her. "The picture from Africa has a drum. Do you have a picture with something that makes music?"

Opportunities for Cooperation

Before the children put the pictures back in the basket, the assistant teacher asks them to take a good look at the long row of pictures on the floor. There are families from all over the world. How are they alike? As the children talk about the ways in which the families are alike, they are beginning to define family in a way they can understand. Families eat together, play together, live together, and celebrate together.

Variations

All Kinds of Families, written by Norma Simon, is a delightful book that describes different family structures and different patterns of family life. Rather than reading the book to children in one sitting, select a few pages to read at a time and use these pages as the basis of class projects and activities. Concepts related to family that could be reinforced or expanded include the following:

▼ Families come in all sizes and in all ages.

▼ A family is people who belong together.

▼ Families share good times and bad times.

▼ When families get together, they talk a lot, they eat a lot, and they laugh a lot.

▼ Some people in a family may live in different places. They are still a family.

▼ Families share stories and tell them many times.

As the children talk about the ways in which the families are alike, they are beginning to define family in a way they can understand. Families eat together, play together, live together, and celebrate together.

The Classroom as a Family - Classroom Two

After all, families share important things with each other, and if you're a preschool child, your name in print is something very important.

The Scene

In preparation for circle time, the teacher has placed two large trays in the center of the circle. One tray is filled with polaroid pictures of the children in the class, with picture side down and the name of each child printed on the back. The second tray is empty.

A Sample Script

"We are going to play a guessing game today," begins the teacher. "When I pass the tray around, you point to one of the pictures and tell me whose picture you think it is. Turn the picture over. If you guess right, take the picture out and put it in the second tray. Then give the child beside you a turn to choose a picture. How long do you think it will take us to get all the pictures on the second tray?"

"Can we choose our own pictures?" one child asks. "If you want to," the teacher replies, "but it may be more fun to find a picture of one of your friends. Dominic, why don't you begin?"

"I found me," Dominic announces proudly, after taking a quick peek at several of the pictures. He shows his photo to the class and sets it down in the second tray with a self-satisfied grin. Next, it is Paul's turn. Paul finds a photo with "Paul" written on it and picks it up confidently. "No fair, it's not me," he whines when he turns the picture over. The teacher intervenes, "Remember, there are two Pauls in this class. You found the other Paul's picture and you were right—it is a picture of Paul, so put the picture in the second tray."

The game continues until all the pictures have been moved from the first tray to the second tray. During the first go around each child chooses, or at least tries to choose, his or her own picture. Knowing that Phillipa has not learned to recognize her name, the teacher gives her the last turn so that she can be successful. After playing the game a few times, the children begin to choose their friend's name.

Variations

When the children have learned to read each other's names, their feeling of being part of a family is strengthened. After all, families share important things with each other, and if you're a preschool child, your name in print is something very important.

Another circle time activity that strengthens the spirit of family is a category game. A simple version of the category game is an activity record like Hap Palmer's "Reds Stand Up." When all the children wearing red stand up, or all the children wearing yellow, children are learning in a subtle way that members of the classroom family, like members of their own families, are alike in some ways and different in other ways. Once children have learned a category game, teachers and children can introduce interesting variations. Everybody stand up who has a brother, everybody stand up who had oatmeal for breakfast, everybody with buttons on their shirt touch your ears. As the category games get more complicated, children spend more time looking at each other and discovering likes and differences.

▼ Birthday Celebrations

The anticipation of a birthday can be just as exciting as the celebration. Classroom teachers can help make children's birthdays a special event by posting all the children's birthdays on the wall, with a very special place reserved for the birthday of the week. A birthday train works very well with the birthday of the week positioned in the front of the train.

▼ Classroom Projects

When the whole class participates in a class project, the feeling of being part of a family is strengthened. Class projects can be quite simple—preparing breakfast in the classroom or sending a get-well card to a classmate—or quite elaborate and creative. One project that has worked well in preschool classrooms is making a collection and setting up a classroom museum. Buttons, rocks, tops of containers, nails and screws, postcards, or different kinds of string can become intriguing collections. And of course, the most-fun part of making a collection is setting up a display and opening the classroom to visitors.

▼ Coat of Arms

Just the way families have a coat of arms that reflects family history, children can create a classroom coat of arms that represents their classroom. Cut a crest out of poster paper and divide it into four quadrants. Help the children decide what symbol to place in each quadrant. Typically, a class may choose a sketch of a classroom pet, an item from their classroom collection, a bus ticket from a field trip, and a pressed flower from a nature walk.

▼ Service Projects

When a class assumes a shared responsibility like taking care of a pet, making holiday decorations for the children's wing in a hospital, or drawing pictures for children who lost their home in a hurricane, the classroom bond is strengthened. Children recognize in a concrete way that by working together, family style, they can do things that are meaningful and important. In selecting class service projects, it is important to find a project where children can understand the need and recognize their ability to help.

▼ Class Beautification

When children assume ownership of their classroom, family feelings are enhanced. Although it is tempting for teachers to reserve teacher work days for major cleanings and reorganizations, children's feelings of ownership are better served when the children are involved in its beautification. One way to get children involved in class beautification is to put them in charge of clean-up. A more powerful way is to let the children cooperate on a project that adds to the "decor" of the classroom. Possible projects include growing class plants and putting them on a window sill, bordering the parent bulletin board with a frame made out of soda can tabs, or decorating a pretend window in the housekeeping corner with "hand-crafted" paper flowers.

▼ Patchwork Quilt

A patchwork quilt is a relatively easy art project that almost all children enjoy. Write each child's name on a square of colored construction paper. Hang a large sheet of paper on the wall. Give each child the square of paper with his or her name on it. Suggest to the children that they draw a design on the paper—flowers, colored dots, miniature collages, or whatever they choose. Paste each of the squares on the wall hanging to create a family patchwork quilt.

▼ Classroom Family Albums or Flip Charts

Whether you use an album or a flip chart, keeping a photo record of classroom events is a delightful activity. Children love the idea of taking pictures and telling stories of special events and field trips, and once the album is put together, it becomes a favorite classroom resource. When the album is placed in the language corner, children will "read" it over and over again, sharing memories and giggling about things that happened. On a parent night, teachers and children can use their album as an informal way of sharing happenings with parents, or as the basis of a more formal classroom production.

▼ Photo Collages

A photo collage that includes a photo of every child in the class-room is a graphic way of recognizing that the classroom is a family. It is a daily reminder that every child in the class belongs and that no one can be excluded.

▼ Routines and Traditions

Just the way a family develops traditions that support cohesiveness, every classroom develops its own special traditions that give it a family identity. In some classes, the tradition could be as simple as a special kind of wave that the class invents to greet each other in the morning. It can also be more elaborate, like making a tape of favorite family songs and playing it every Friday. One tradition that works for many classrooms is holding classroom meetings. Classroom meetings can be held for many different purposes—for planning a special event, for generating a set of classroom rules, or for dealing with a problem situation.

It is especially important to give a family meeting structure, so that it is not perceived of as simply another circle time.

- Limit the "agenda" of the meeting to one salient item and state the agenda at the beginning of the meeting.
- Set ground rules for the meeting—such as everybody gets a turn giving their opinion. No one can interrupt or make fun of another child's ideas.
- Appoint a "scribe" who will take down the minutes of the meeting. (A teacher assistant makes a good scribe.)
- Review the outcome of the meeting before the meeting comes to an end.
- Set the meeting up in a special place—a corner of the playground, a school office, or a section of the classroom set aside for meetings.
- Provide a way of signaling the beginning and the end of the class-room meeting—such as a gavel or a bell.

DEVELOPING SOCIAL SKILLS

In the first 10 chapters of *Play Together, Grow Together*, we have identified ways of infusing cooperative goals into the preschool program. In this chapter, our focus shifts from the content of the curriculum to the role of the teacher. During a large part of the day, the role of the teacher in a cooperative classroom is that of interested observer. When the classroom runs smoothly and children play happily together, the teacher steps aside and observes the interactions. When trouble brews in the classroom, when children act unkindly and bad feelings emerge, the teacher assumes a more active role. But whether the teacher is observing quietly or intervening actively, the teacher is the cogwheel of a cooperative classroom. In this chapter, we look at three critical challenges facing the classroom teacher.

- Reducing and resolving conflict situations

- Helping individual children who have problems with social skills

- Enhancing prosocial behaviors

CHALLENGE ONE: REDUCING AND RESOLVING CONFLICT

Preschool teachers, like other authority figures, try to manage conflict by setting rules. Some rules prohibit specific forms of conflict, such as biting. When one of these rules is broken, the teacher may feel that cooperation is served by firm discipline. Strong disapproval is directed toward the aggressor, and frequently it is couched in distinctive language. Instead of saying, "You cannot bite," teachers say, "You *may* not bite." Instead of saying, "You have to stop biting," they say, "You *need* to stop biting." These unusual verb forms, spoken in a serious tone of voice, catch the attention of the children and alert them to the fact that the teacher means business. In addition, children who break a rule like "No biting" may be required to sit

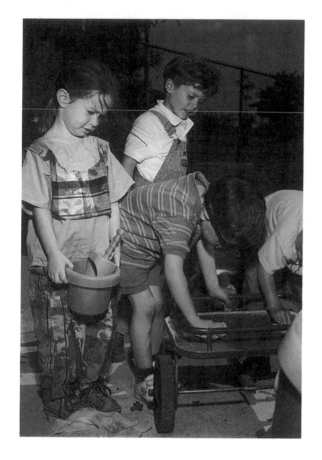

Resolving conflict in preschool classroom becomes a teaching/learning process, an opportunity for teachers to help children learn the social skills and attitudes they need for cooperative interaction.

in a timeout chair. In short, the orientation of teachers in this kind of situation is to impress upon children the unyielding quality of certain rules.

At the other extreme, every teacher operates with rules that permit some forms of conflict. For example, a child generally is allowed to take the role of a monster and chase other children, assuming there is a safe place to hold the activity and the monster does not get carried away. In this kind of situation, teachers are reluctant to intervene because they feel children need to learn how to cope on their own with a limited amount of conflict.

Between these two extremes lies a vast number of situations that are less clear. The conflicts that arise are not so serious that a teacher immediately resorts to strong disapproval and punishment. At the same time, these conflicts are not so minor that a teacher overlooks them. The teacher feels that the children need some adult guidance, but the manner and extent of this guidance is highly variable. With children who have trouble resolving conflict in a cooperative spirit, the teacher tends to intervene more quickly and decisively. With children who are socially skilled, the teacher's intervention is more likely to be tentative and indirect.

Teachers make these judgements in an instant and often are not even aware of their thought process. But in each case they are trying to strike a balance between too much interference and too little. On the one hand, they want children to learn how to resolve their own problems, while on the other hand, they want children to treat each other with kindness and fairness. The teacher who stresses cooperation will be especially concerned about this balance because cooperative play requires both of these contrasting goals. Children who cooperate need the ability to organize and regulate their own play. They also need to be sensitive to the needs of other children. In other words, children need to learn self reliance and consideration.

Viewed within this kind of framework, resolving conflict in preschool classroom becomes a teaching/learning process, an opportunity for teachers to help children learn the social skills and attitudes they need for cooperative interaction. Except in extreme circumstances, the process is more important than the immediate results. Resolution of a conflict is desirable, but even more desirable is interaction between teachers and children that promotes social growth. How does this interaction take place? What are the techniques that teachers can use? In sharing their views with us, experienced teachers stressed again and again the need to be flexible. No one approach is effective all the time, and therefore these teachers find it necessary to develop a variety of techniques and to remain open to new suggestions. We have grouped these ideas into three categories and have related several anecdotes within each of the categories:

1. Focusing on Feelings
2. Focusing on Clear Communication
3. Teaching New Kinds of Behaviors

As we read the anecdotes provided by three different teachers, we recognize that the approach they select meets the demands of the situation and reflects the teacher's style and personality.

Focusing on Feelings

Teachers agree that it is important to respond to a conflict situation by encouraging the participants to express their feelings. An expression of feelings often clears the air, or at least points the way toward a solution. When children tell each other how they feel, they may begin to see each other's perspective and respond with a degree of empathy.

Teachers agree that it is important to respond to a conflict situation by encouraging the participants to express their feelings.

▼ The Matter of Fact Style

I pride myself on being able to watch a whole classroom of children and know what is going on. When a child gets upset, I usually have a pretty good idea why, but I would rather have the child tell me what is wrong. I might go up to the child and say, "What's wrong?" or "Why are you so angry?" I use direct, common sense questions. In a group situation I do the same thing. I ask each child to explain what the problem is before we try to solve it. Of course, I make sure ahead of time that I know what has happened. Then if the children report different facts, I'm in a position to say, "Well, this is what I saw going on." I think there is a temptation to rush into a conflict situation and start looking right away for the solution. But if you begin by giving children a chance to put their feelings on the table, it's surprising how often a problem just melts away. Or some solution pops up in the statements of the children...

▼ The Nurturant Style

As a child I was quiet and shy. I am really bothered when children say things to each other that are mean. So I work hard trying to get the children to express their feelings in gentle ways. When someone says, "We're not your friend," I point out that words like that hurt people's feelings. And I suggest different words, "I'm playing with Melanie right now, when I'm finished maybe I can play with you." If someone says, "I hate you," I'm likely to join the conversation and say, "I would

How children express their feelings in a conflict situation will establish a certain pattern of communication. If the pattern of communication promotes mutual respect, it probably will prove productive and the dispute will be settled amicably. If the pattern of communication makes one or both parties feel belittled, the conflict probably will worsen.

prefer you didn't talk that way. You can say, 'You play too rough,' or 'You won't share,' instead of, 'I hate you'." I talk to the children about the difference between friendly teasing and mean teasing. Friendly teasing, I tell them, makes you feel happy inside. It makes you feel like smiling and laughing. But mean teasing makes you feel bad inside. You want to cry or hit someone. I also give children words to protect themselves from mean teasing, like "I'm not listening to you," or "I know that's not true." I don't expect them to adopt my language. Usually they learn to protect themselves by saying, "So what?" or "Who cares?" or "You liar."   But even if the children don't use my words, I believe that when I model gentle language they become more aware of other people's feelings...

▼ The Playful Style

When children have trouble with sharing or waiting for turns I try to focus on how they feel rather than what they've done wrong. Here's an example of a conversation I had with Jeremy when he grabbed a funnel from another child.

"Jeremy, I know you really wanted that funnel but Josie had it first. I'll tell you what. Give the funnel back to Josie and you and I will play a funnel game. Are you ready?

I want that funnel, I really do,

So I'll pretend I have one too."

Jeremy had a great time pretending he had the funnel. As a matter of fact, several other children joined the game.

Focusing on Clear Communication

In the following excerpts we look at the same three teachers as they stress the importance of clear communication. How children express their feelings in a conflict situation will establish a certain pattern of communication. If the pattern of communication promotes mutual respect, it probably will prove productive and the dispute will be settled amicably. If the pattern of communication makes one or both parties feel belittled, the conflict probably will worsen. As the teachers in this section make clear, good communication involves skills that teachers can model and explain.

▼ A Matter-of-Fact Style

Ideally, I believe conflict should be resolved by talking things out. As long as children are talking to each other, even if the conversation is getting a little rough around the edges, there is a good chance of settling a dispute. Nearly every year I have a child who continually grabs things from other children, or a child who reacts to social frustration by screaming. These are the children who don't know how to use language in order to solve their conflicts. I realize how important it is to help the children recognize the power of words and to use words to make their wishes known.

Let me give you an example. In my Tuesday-Thursday class the grabber is named Brad. Yesterday he tried to grab a walkie-talkie from Tony. I immediately asked Brad, "Do you want to play with the walkie-talkie?" He mumbled something that sounded affirmative. "Then," I said, "You need to tell Tony: I would like to play with the walkie-talkie." Brad just stood there, looking at Tony. I continued to direct Brad, "You can't take the toy away from Tony, but you can ask him for a turn." Still nothing from Brad. I tried again, "Ask Tony if you can play with the walkie-talkie when he's finished." This particular incident ended when Tony put the toy radio down and went off to play somewhere else, but I felt some progress occurred. A little later, I observed Brad asking another child for a ball.

Negotiating for turns is hard for preschool children, and I don't try to push it too far. But every once in a while I see a good chance to slip it in.

With some children, no matter how hard I try, it's really tough to get through. They have gotten into the habit of grabbing and screaming and the polite words don't come easily. But being on the scene at the right time and helping children find the right words eventually makes a difference.

▼ The Nurturant Style

In our classroom, we follow the usual rule about sharing and taking turns. If one child is busy playing with a toy and does not want any help, other children must wait until that child is finished playing. The trouble comes when the children are not clear about the ending of one turn and the beginning of another. For example, on our playground the children like to turn somersaults on a low bar. They have to take turns because there's really only room for one child at a time, but it's not clear when each turn is over. In this situation, I try to show the children how they can communicate with each other and solve the problem. I demonstrate by asking the child at the bar, "How many somersaults do you want to do?" After setting on a reasonable number, I suggest that the children waiting in line help by counting the somersaults. In a way I am teaching the children how to negotiate a contract. Naturally some of the children pick up the idea faster than others— maybe they will be the lawyers and politicians of the future.

Negotiating for turns is hard for preschool children, and I don't try to push it too far. But every once in a while I see a good chance to slip it in. When we first put a Sit and Spin toy in the classroom, everyone wanted to ride on it. I encouraged the children to decide how many times around each child would go. I've also tried this technique when children are having a hard time sharing the tricycles. Often the children forget to make a deal ahead of time and then begin the negotiation process at a later point. One child comes up to another and matter of factly says, "You've had that trike a long time—it's my turn now." Surprisingly, even this negotiation after the fact is very effective...

▼ The Playful Style

In a conflict situation, my first goal is to get children to talk to each other. Of course, sometimes the conflict has gone too far for talking. But there is a talking phase in most fights between preschool children, and this is the point at which I try to intervene. During the talking phase, the children threaten and insult each other. As the argument escalates, the children become too angry to communicate with each other, but they still are capable of talking to a third party. In fact, they want to communicate with me in order to win my support. If I join the scene, I have to be careful to avoid playing the role of an arbitrator—at least at first. Instead, my role is to be a mediator. I'm like a special,

Sometimes conflict can be resolved by persuading children to avoid a confrontation. Children can change their perception of a situation and with it their feeling that a problem exists.

diplomatic telephone—one that faithfully transmits messages but at the same time removes abusive and provocative language. I am a device to reestablish communication between two individuals who are so involved in shouting and whining that they do not hear each other.

The other day Marvin threatened Serina, "Give me that ball or I'll kick you." I was in a position to mediate. Seeing Serina was preparing to resist, I said to her, "Marvin says he wants a turn with the ball..."

"Well, he can't have it," Serina retorted, adding, "He's a dummy." Turning to Marvin I reported, "Serina says she's using the ball now." Speaking to me, Marvin justified his request, "But I want to throw the ball against the wall." Serina responded, "That's what I'm going to do too." It is important to stay with the mediation process until the antagonists can clearly see their own way to a solution, but at this point I withdrew, thinking that Marvin and Serina would join together in a game of ball-against-the-wall. And that is exactly what happened.

Teaching a New Set of Behaviors

Sometimes conflict can be resolved by persuading children to avoid a confrontation. Children can change their perception of a situation and with it their feeling that a problem exists. Trying to avoid conflict is not a passive strategy on the part of teachers, but a very active one in which teachers call upon their own creativity and enlist the creativity of children as well. Once drawn into the creative process, angry feelings disappear and children can go back to enjoying some level of cooperative play.

Let us listen again to our three teachers as they describe situations in which they introduced a new set of bahaviors.

▼ The Matter of Fact Style

I feel that some conflict situations can be handled best by introducing a new idea. This is particularly true when the children involved in the conflict have become fixated on a limited set of alternatives. For example, the most popular toy in my classroom is a kind of bus, a four-foot-long board with wheels. The children can propel it with their feet, and it is an ideal toy for two children to share. But if both children want to be the driver, there is bound to be a conflict. One solution is to take turns, but I prefer to expand the play ideas of the children. If the passenger riding in the back can find something to do that is just as appealing as driving, the conflict will disappear.

I try to show the children that they can create these new ideas themselves. I might say to two children who are arguing about driving, "I know you both want to drive, but let's think of something fun for the

As adults, it is easy for us to think of new ideas that would enrich the play of young children and reduce conflict. The trick, however, is to present the ideas in a way that is acceptable.

person in the back to do." If they have trouble thinking of something, I suggest ideas I have seen other children carrying out. For example, the passenger may be in charge of a wire basket full of cardboard tubes. The children like to pretend that the tubes are hot dogs, bugles, or casts for broken arms. The child in the back may use a pair of binoculars while riding, or pretend to take pictures with a camera. Simply suggesting that the passenger use one of these popular props is often enough to give the children a more concrete idea for their play and to resolve the fixation over who gets to drive the bus.

▼ The Nurturant Style

As adults, it is easy for us to think of new ideas that would enrich the play of young children and reduce conflict. The trick, however, is to present the ideas in a way that is acceptable. I have found that if I suggest a new play idea too directly the children resist it, even though later they may come back to it. On the other hand, if I suggest an idea too casually, it often is lost in the general hubbub. Several years ago, I began to use a specific technique for presenting new play ideas. I told the children that I used to play in this way, or that way, when I was a little girl.

For example, let's say two children are arguing over who gets to be the mother in the playhouse. My approach would be to say, "Well, when I was a little girl, we had a Mama in the family and a Grandma— it would be nice to have a Grandma in your family." Or I might say, "When I was a little girl, I liked to play the Mama, but I really liked to play the big sister; big sisters get to go to school by themselves, and to the movies, and swimming."

The truth is that I don't mind making up all sorts of stories about what I did or felt as a child. Some of the other teachers raise their eyebrows when they hear my little white lies. They refer to my technique as "unorthodox." But I see no harm in it. By being presented as personal memories, my play ideas are taken seriously by the children, and yet the children do not seem to feel I am telling them how to play. I can resolve the conflicts with a simple fiction about my own childhood. And who knows? You can't remember everything from your early years anyway—maybe things really happened the way I imagine them.

▼ The Playful Style

When I first started teaching preschool children, I was shocked by the amount of exclusion that took place in the classroom. Gradually, I realized that excluded children were not as devastated as I would have been. And I began to see that over a period of two or three years, the children steadily learned to include a greater number of peers in their play. Still, I find myself especially concerned about helping children make progress in this direction. Experience has taught me that it does no good to try to force a group to accept another child, but from time to time I demonstrate to the children that their play can become more inclusive. I do this by joining the play myself. Temporarily I become the play group leader, but only long enough to stretch the social vision of the children. Then I fade out and let the level of cooperation resume its normal level. Usually this level is lower than when I was the leader, but higher than before I intervened.

I suppose I get involved most often in the housekeeping area. So often, pretend families are ruthless in their exclusion of other children. I may enter the play as a repairman or a salesman or a delivery person. A child who has been rejected by the family will be my assistant. Together we gain entrance to the pretend family's inner sanctum—whatever it is. Then I demonstrate how outsiders, such as myself and the rejected child, can join the play without disturbing the integrity of the family group. We might repair something and then leave, or sell something and then leave, or deliver something and then leave. In this way the family does not have to accept us as family members but we are included in the play.

The kind of conflict produced by exclusion takes many forms, and I don't try to resolve all of them. But when I see a recurrent situation, I put on my thinking cap and try to come up with a creative solution. I look for a solution I can model by playing with children. If this solution makes enough sense to the children, it will be modified and elaborated by their own creativity.

CHALLENGE TWO: HELPING INDIVIDUAL CHILDREN WHO HAVE PROBLEMS WITH SOCIAL SKILLS

In most situations, an experienced teacher committed to cooperation develops a repertoire of strategies for handling the minor conflicts that arise in a preschool classroom. A more difficult challenge for classroom teachers is working with children who are having difficulty with socialization behaviors; children who are angry, defiant, or aggressive; children who are shy and non-assertive; or out-of-step children who attempt to make friends but are never completely successful.

The Angry, Defiant, and/or Aggressive Child

Children who are angry, defiant, and/or aggressive are a challenge for even the most experienced teacher. Teachers become anxious when children are out of control and may feel themselves responding with anger when children hurt other children.

Most of the time, teachers overcome their own feelings of anger and anxiety. They are able to see that a child who loses self-control is not necessarily rebelling against adult authority or headed for a life of crime. In fact, teachers can sometimes see a positive side to aggressive behavior. In the give and take of peer play, children need to be able to stand up for themselves. The line between being assertive and being aggressive is often a fine one, and a moderate degree of aggression is associated with outgoingness. Preschool children who readily interact with others are bound to get into fights from time to time.

When children are perceived as being overly aggressive, however, negative feelings of anger and anxiety can return to teachers in full force. Their initial revulsion toward acts of aggression is rekindled, and they are apt to lose sight of the children's redeeming characteristics. In short, teachers find themselves disliking these children. In thinking about how overly aggressive children can be helped, teachers need to start by examining their own negative feelings. Are they exaggerating a child's aggressiveness and already projecting failure for this child in future years?

Having tried to place their negative feelings in perspective, teachers are in a better position to think about why a child is acting so aggressively. The first hypothesis teachers usually consider is that the child is having trouble

The line between being assertive and being aggressive is often a fine one, and a moderate degree of aggression is associated with outgoingness.

at home. Conflict with parents or conflict with siblings (which also involves parents) is presumed to be causing excessive feelings of anger. In turn, these feelings of anger are redirected at children and adults in the preschool classroom.

In many cases, teachers see indirect evidence that supports this hypothesis. For one thing, the negative behavior of aggressive children is often not provoked by anything at school. It is as if the children come to school with feelings of resentment and then act aggressively in order to ensure their rejection by teachers and peers. For another thing, the aggression of these children is unpredictable. They may be relatively calm for several weeks and then suddenly turn violent. Their erratic behavior suggests that something beyond the classroom environment is influencing the level of aggression.

If teachers suspect a problem at home, they can offer assistance. They may be able to gain the confidence of parents and help them accept professional counseling. In the classroom, they may be able to talk to aggressive children about their home life. However, the primary responsibility of teachers is to help aggressive children cope with the classroom situation. The relationships that these children develop with classmates will either reduce or compound their problems. Teachers may have little power to change an aggressive child's family life, but they are in a good position to improve the quality of the child's school experience. In order to do so, they need to go beyond speculations about a child's family problems. They must find ways of helping the child maintain control at school. They must protect the other children in the classroom against the aggressive child. They must keep the destructive child from destroying the classroom property. And, most important, they must help the out-of-control child interact with other children in a mutually satisfactory way.

Ways of helping the out-of-control child can be grouped under the following headings:

1. Attach negative consequences to negative behavior
2. Redirect negative behavior
3. Provide a cool-down period
4. Reward positive behavior
5. Help the child achieve social goals in a nonaggressive way

▼ Attaching Negative Consequences to Negative Behavior

Most preschool children do not like children who are aggressive or destructive and do not want to play with them. Because most preschool children are seeking playmates, we could conclude that there is a built-in negative consequence for out-of-control behavior, which can operate without teacher intervention.

Most preschool children do not like children who are aggressive or destructive and do not want to play with them.

Whatever the reason for a child's aggression, it is important for the child to learn that aggressive behavior has negative consequences. The negative consequence that naturally occurs is that other children do not want to play with an aggressor.

Unfortunately, when children are out of control, a different set of dynamics is in operation. The out-of-control child hits another child. The child reacts with anger, hitting back or running off to another friend. The out-of-control child reacts with escalated anger and the aggression becomes more intense.

While out-of-control children are rejected by their peers when they are overtly aggressive, they are not necessarily social outcasts. As a matter of fact, some aggressive children have considerable leadership ability and relatively high status; some have a modest level of leadership ability and status; some have little leadership ability and very low status. Clearly these different kinds of children do not have the same classroom experiences.

Children with leadership ability are often accepted by others, at least momentarily. Because of their dominance, they tend to express aggressive behavior in the form of cruelty. This cruelty is more than an outburst of anger; it is a way of maintaining control. Sometimes such children establish relationships in which they regularly exploit other children.

At the other extreme, aggressive children with very little leadership ability are rarely accepted in peer play. Their classroom experience is one of almost total rejection. They know they are unlikable, and their aggressive behavior reflects a deep sense of frustration and unhappiness.

In between are children who enjoy a moderate degree of social success. Their aggressiveness is not associated either with the pleasure of being cruel or the frustration of being left out. Instead it seems to be linked to feelings of insecurity. Of course, it can be argued that all aggressive children feel insecure, but these particular children appear to have an especially low tolerance of peer rejection. They overreact when other children either ignore them or refuse to play with them. In reality, they are accepted much of the time, but apparently this does not help them tolerate nonacceptance.

When planning how to help aggressive children, teachers can adjust their behavior to these individual differences. If a child exhibits leadership ability, it probably will be important to break the connection between leadership and cruelty. This kind of child needs to learn that leadership becomes more powerful when it is not coupled with aggression. If an aggressive child has very low status with peers, the teacher will want to concentrate on helping the child develop a more positive self-image. Finding just one or two friends is a worthy goal for this kind of child. If an aggressive child seems unusually sensitive to peer rejection and is trying to compensate by attaching himself to a dominant child, the teacher can focus on building up the child's sense of self reliance. With the teacher's help, this kind of child may eventually become a leader of modest proportions.

Whatever the reason for a child's aggression, it is important for the child to learn that aggressive behavior has negative consequences. The negative consequence that naturally occurs is that other children do not want to play with an aggressor. It may help for the teacher to call attention to this fact. However, in many cases, rejection by other children makes an aggressive child more angry. In order to turn around the negative spiral of rejection and aggression, teachers often intervene and set a consequence for aggressive behavior.

The most commonly used negative consequence theory is a time-out procedure. "Time-out" serves as a safety valve for aggressive children. It provides a cooling off period and protects angry children from each other. At the same time, time-out is a clear statement to everyone in the class that causing hurt to other children is simply not acceptable.

Having made time-out the "natural" consequence of aggression, the teacher hopes to reduce the tendency of other children to reject an aggressive peer. In effect, the teacher is saying to the children: "If I make an aggressive child go to time-out, that is sufficient punishment; now let us try to accept this child in our play." Such a solution is much easier to state than to put into practice. The aggressive child may still be rejected by others; the aggressive child may persist in being aggressive. In itself, a timeout procedure, or some other punishment, is not likely to be enough to help aggressive children develop social skills.

▼ Redirecting Negative Behavior

Recognizing that the turning point for the aggressive child is the discovery that playing with other children is fun, many teachers focus on engineering the environment so that aggressive children can expend their energy in a socially desirable way. Let us listen to an experienced teacher describe a redirection technique.

You can guess pretty well in advance that if these children engage in active group play—like building a structure with large blocks or riding trikes on the playground—somebody is bound to get hurt. What I try to do is redirect their energies before they get aggressive. I might say to the child who is about to knock a block structure down,

"That's a great block house. Can you make it even higher?" Or if the child is about to crash into another child with a tricycle, I might say, "Whoa there, we need a safety scout. Jump off your tricycle and run around the playground to make sure that there's nothing dangerous." Naturally, those strategies don't always work, but after a while at least some of the aggressive children see themselves in a helper role.

▼ Providing Private "Cool Down" Time with Teachers

While redirection works well with some children, some out-of-control children require a different approach. Let us listen to a teacher discuss a cool down procedure.

> Like other teachers, I believe in acknowledging a child's feelings of anger and redirecting them, but my style is different. With a child who is very aggressive, I prefer to lead the child away from the peer group and talk privately, one to one. I feel the child listens better and is less likely to show off by being defiant. When we're out of the fray, I look for an activity that will calm the child. I've had good luck reading stories to aggressive children. That often seems to sooth their angry feelings, and I think they enjoy the physical contact of sitting close to me. If I don't have time to read a story, I suggest the child sit in the reading corner and listen to a taped story. I usually have a special tape up my sleeve for this kind of child.
>
> I suppose a person could say that I'm rewarding children for being aggressive, but I don't look at it that way. I feel that aggressive children get a steady diet of negative attention, both at home and at school, and that any positive attention will reduce their antisocial behavior. Naturally, I encourage angry children to cool off in the reading corner before they reach the boiling point. And over time I do see them looking at books and listening to taped stories on their own.

▼ Rewarding Positive Behavior

A favored technique for helping children who are having difficulty with self-control is rewarding positive behavior. The "catch the child being good" technique is based on the theory that behaviors are reinforced or strengthened by their consequences. In other words, if we praise a child when he is behaving in a socially appropriate way, it will increase the probability that this socially appropriate behavior will reoccur. Positive reinforcement can be used successfully in conjunction with other approaches. Let us listen to an experienced teacher describe a technique she uses to reward positive behavior.

A favored technique for helping children who are having difficulty with self-control is rewarding positive behavior. The "catch the child being good" technique is based on the theory that behaviors are reinforced or strengthened by their consequences.

I favor ignoring aggressive behavior and giving attention to the victim. However, at the same time, you need to set up a behavior modification program for the aggressive child. If you just try to ignore the child's meanness, the child will get more and more violent until finally he gets your attention. After all, this kind of child expects to get attention by being aggressive, and he can escalate his attacks if you don't respond. But if you work out a reward system for good bahavior, while you try to ignore aggression, then you may be able to turn things around.

When I talk about a reward system I don't mean anything that's really formal or overstructured. I don't have the time or, I guess, the discipline to carry out a formal plan. What I do try to do is catch the child being good—and then I give her a word of praise or a quick hug rather than a tangible reward. With some children, this approach doesn't work, but for the most part I've been pretty successful.

THE SHY OR NONASSERTIVE CHILD

Allison and Carmen were sitting at the craft table preparing a plate of tiny clay cookies for Goofy's birthday party. Molly arrived at the table and edged in between the two girls.

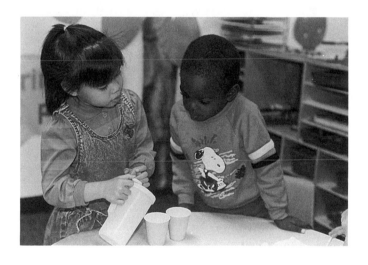

"I can make cookies too," she boasted, placing a large slab of clay in the center of the plate.

"You're messing up our cookies," Allison shouted. "Get away from here."

"Yeh, get away from here," Carmen echoed, shoving Molly off with her elbow.

For some children, friend making is an automatic and unlearned bahavior. These children approach potential playmates with enthusiasm, fully confident that they will be accepted. If the child they select doesn't want to play with them, they take it in stride and go off to find a new prospect. For other children, making friends is a much more difficult feat. Some children are so fearful of rejection that they will not risk an approach. Other children try to make friends, but their approach is so tentative that other childen ignore or reject them.

In contrast to their reactions to an aggressive child, most teachers are drawn to the shy and nonassertive child. They recognize that nonassertive children are likely to be gentle and empathetic, and, once they form a friendship, they are likely to maintain it. Here are some techniques that teachers have described for helping the child who is shy.

▼ Shy Child Paired with Another

Antonia is a particularly small child from a bilingual home. Although her English is pretty good, she almost never talks in circle time, and during free play, she is off by herself, doing a puzzle or perhaps just watching the other children.

My first approach was to give Antonia opportunities to do special things like giving out the cookies at snack time or passing out the crayons. This didn't work at all. When one child complained about getting the smallest cookie, Antonia was close to tears. My second idea worked out much better. I chose Antonia and Carmen to be my helpers for the day. Carmen is a delightfully friendly child and all the children love to play with her. She initiated a conversation with Antonia as they wiped off the tables, and Antonia beamed with pleasure. The other children took their lead from Carmen. By the end of the day, Antonia was in the housekeeping corner with several other children. She will always be on the shy side, that's just her temperament, but she is beginning to make friends.

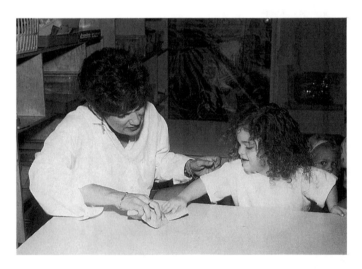

▼ Giving the Shy Child an Edge

I've noticed that children who are feeling uncomfortable play in certain parts of the classroom. Take the puzzles, for example. I don't know how many times I've seen new children gravitate toward the puzzles. Then, when they feel more comfortable, they branch out. But the really shy children are still there—quietly doing the puzzles. I can understand that. Doing a puzzle is a good way to keep busy by yourself, and puzzles don't talk back. You get the feeling you've accomplished something without having to deal with other children. Or maybe a shy child ends up standing around the arts and crafts area or the Play-Doh table. The pattern is not always the same, but in each case the shy child finds a kind of play that does not require much face-to-face interaction.

My approach is to accept this pattern and go from there. I think to myself: Is there a way to make interaction more likely in that spot? I try to give a shy child some extra edge, some favorable position, that will encourage the other children to seek him out. Let's say the child is hiding out in the puzzle area. I might find a new puzzle for the classroom and casually give it to the shy child first. That way he gets first crack at it—and maybe, just maybe, the next child to play with it will need some help, and a little bit of friendly interaction takes place. Or if the child tends to be around the crafts area, I might quietly ask him to be my helper. I'll come up with a job that looks prestigious, like dropping the colored tablets into the bowl of water when we dye Easter eggs. Maybe, just maybe, this shy child will be so proud of his job that he will talk to someone about it. Or other children will be so impressed with him that they will start a conversation.

Finding little ways, as often as possible, to tip the balance in favor of a shy child—that's how I try to break down the barrier of shyness.

▼ Teaching the Shy Child Social Skills

I feel shy children simply don't know how to get started, and the most straightforward technique is to tell them. First, I observe a shy child in order to find out what she is watching in the classroom. Then I invite the child to sit down with me and we watch together. We find an observation post that is close enough to see what is happening but far enough away to be private. As we sit together, I sometimes ask the child what she sees; mostly I tell her what I see. What I see is pretty much the same—children who want to play together and who do certain things to get the play started and to keep it going.

> Look. Stacy wants to play with Angela, so she's giving Angela a toy. Did you see what the toy was?...

> Now Deanna wants to play too. Look, she's smiling at Angela, and she's standing close to Angela. I wonder if Angela will let her play?...

> What's Deanna doing now? She's copying Stacy. She's doing exactly the same thing—crawling under the table and out on the other side. They're all laughing...

> Now Deanna wants to dress up like Stacy. But look, first she's asking Angela if it's alright. Angela said yes.

Eventually I become more directive in my comments, suggesting ways that the shy child might join in. My major goal, however, is still to describe in words the social skills of the children we are watching.

I'm not sure shy children actually learn these skills by talking about them—I rather doubt it. I think they gain the confidence to try out skills they already possess. After all, most preschool children come to school with a wealth of social skills that have been learned at home. Whatever the reason, talking about what is happening helps shy children make the transition from watching to interacting.

▼ The Out-of-Step Child

The out-of-step child is the socially awkward child who wants to make friends very badly, but goes about it in the wrong way, Some out-of-step children play the clown in order to attract attention—making silly faces, belching loudly, or mocking another child. Other children who are socially awkward fail to read social cues. They continue to pester a child who has made it clear that he doesn't want to play and then miss an opportunity to join a group because they were waiting for an invitation. Since the socially awkward child has difficulty reading social cues, direct instruction is usually the best approach.

> I have this child, Carlos, in my class who's a really neat kid, but he just doesn't know how to play with other children. Sometimes he tries to get their attention by acting a like a clown, throwing his hat up in the air or burping in everyone's face and the children are really turned off. At other times, he'll go up to a group that is busy playing and ask if he can play, too. Unfortunately, the children are quite likely to say, "No, you can't. Go away."

> Before I developed a plan for working with Carlos, I decided to spend a few minutes observing Dominic to see if I could get some pointers. Dominic is the newest boy in the class but he seems to have no trouble gaining acceptance. I watched him one day as he approached three really cliquish boys who were playing in the block area. At first, Dominic just stood in the background and watched the children build. While Dominick was hovering, one child dubbed himself King Polooka and ordered his subjects to build a throne. Dominic seized the moment. "Here, King Palooka. I brought you a brick for your throne." When I looked around a few minutes later, Dominic was happily accepted by the block-building clique. After all, what king would want to ban such a loyal subject?

> I recognized immediately that Carlos could be taught to use Dominic's approach technique. The next day, when Carlos and I were on the playground, a group of children were making a mud castle in the middle of the sandbox. "Queen Genevee" was directing knights to build a moat. Carlos was

---

The out-of-step child is the socially awkward child who wants to make friends very badly, but goes about it in the wrong way.

about to ask if he could play. I whispered to him, "Ask Queen Genevee if she would like a flag for her castle, and give her this stick." Carlos took my advice and it worked. Queen Genevee took the stick from Carlos and the children let him join the group. But the best thing that happened was that Carlos began to trust me. Together we found ways of getting other children to play with him, and the clowning behavior almost disappeared.

CHALLENGE THREE: SUPPORTING EMPATHY, PERSPECTIVE TAKING, HELPFULNESS, AND GENEROSITY

We have been talking in this chapter about ways of helping individual children develop social skills and engage successfully in group play. While it is important for a classroom teacher to identify children who need special help, it is equally important to engage all children in the enhancement of social skills. Children who are empathetic, caring, generous, and helpful flourish in a cooperative classroom.

Developing Empathy

Parents of young children are often amazed at their child's empathic bahaviors. Mothers talk about how their toddlers try to comfort them when they are unhappy, or how their three year old burst into tears when their puppy got a booster shot. A preschooler's capacity for empathy, for recognizing and experiencing the feelings of another person, is used by preschool teachers as the basis for developing more complex social skills.

We have a puppet called Button Eyes who is a permanent resident in our classroom. He greets each child by name when the children come to school in the morning and waves good-bye when they leave in the

While empathy is certainly the starting point for generating prosocial skills, empathy by itself may not lead to helping behavior. In order to be generous or helpful, a child must be able to assume the point of view of another person, to recognize that another person's feelings or desires are not the same as her own.

afternoon. Button Eyes is enormously helpful when it comes to clean-up time. The children know how upset Button Eyes gets when the classroom is messed up. The other day, a piece of puzzle disappeared and the children insisted on finding it before they went out because they didn't want Button Eyes to be sad. Button Eyes is especially useful when it comes to teaching social skills. Let me tell you what happened the other day.

A new girl, Janika, was due to come into the class at snack time. Janika has a congenital deformity and one of her hands lacks fingers. I wanted Janika to feel welcome in the classroom and I wasn't sure how the children would handle the situation. I decided to let Button Eyes help me. When the children came to circle time I started a conversation with Button Eyes.

Teacher:	What's the matter, Button Eyes, you look a little worried?
Button Eyes:	I am worried. Janika is coming to our class and I don't even know her.
Teacher:	Nobody knows Janika yet, but I can tell you about her. Janika is four years old just like you. She has brown eyes and a pony tail, and one of her hands doesn't have any fingers.
Button Eyes:	Oh, dear, something is wrong with her hand. Is it catching?
Teacher:	Button Eyes, you are so silly. Your hands don't look like our hands but your hands are not catching. (The children look at their own hands and start to giggle.)
Button Eyes:	But how can she hold hands at circle time if she doesn't have fingers?
Teacher:	You know what, Button Eyes, let's ask the children, maybe they have some good ideas.

You know, the children were just wonderful. They told Button Eyes that he didn't have to be afraid, that we could hold Janika's arms. Then we got into a wonderful conversation about different kinds of handicaps. The conversation with Button Eyes gave us an opportunity to talk openly about their fears and concerns. When Janika came to the class that day, the children were great. Janika is a terrific kid, and everyone wants to be her friend.

The puppet technique described by this teacher is an excellent way to encourage empathy. It also can be used, as we saw in the above example, as a preventive technique to avert a potential problem. Other techniques that can be used to encourage empathy include doll play, pet care, pretend play with miniature figures, and reading books about feelings.

Perspective Taking and Helping Behavior

While empathy is certainly the starting point for generating prosocial skills, empathy by itself may not lead to helping behavior. In order to be generous or helpful, a child must be able to assume the point of view of another person, to recognize that another person's feelings or desires are not the same as her own. It is not easy for young children to take the perspective of another person. Young children are often described as egocentric, as thinking of themselves as the center of the universe. The moon is following them. It is getting dark outside so they can go to sleep. The egocentrism of the young child is evidenced in the perceptions of the social world as well as the physical world. The two year old gives his mother a pacifier to stop her from crying. The three year old wants to buy her father a panda bear or a ninja turtle. Although children cannot be expected to fully outgrow their egocentric thinking, playing with other children, engaging in pretend play, and assuming the role of another person—"I be the mommy and you be the baby."—allow the children to view reality from a different perspective. Psychodrama, or acting out stories, is an excellent technique used by preschool teachers to develop perspective taking.

Psychodrama, or acting out stories, is an excellent technique used by preschool teachers to develop perspective taking.

The Scene
It is circle time and the teacher is sitting on the floor with ten children around her. A small carton has been placed in the center of the circle. The box contains story props (craft sticks with different faces glued on) that represent characters in *Jack and the Beanstalk.*

A Sample Script
The teacher begins, "Remember yesterday when we decided to write our own story of Jack and the Beanstalk? Jennifer thought that Jack was not very nice when he stole the eggs from the giant. And Pedro thought that the giant was being real mean to Jack and it was okay for Jack to take the golden eggs. So you all decided to tell the story a new way. Well, I liked your way so much that I made ten story puppets so that we could put on our own Jack and the Beanstalk play." At this point the teacher hands

out the props, giving the puppets that do most of the talking to the more verbal children. The props include: Jack, Jack's stepmother, the farmer, the beanstalk, the giant, the giant's wife, the goose, the giant's two children, and a rabbit. (Whoever gets to be the rabbit in the stories always does the prompting.) Because the children are used to putting on plays with story props, they have no difficulty getting started:

Beyond all else, as we look at classrooms in which children have internalized the ideals and values of a cooperative curriculum, we recognize that the teacher, as a model, plays a critical role.

Stepmother:	We don't have any money. (To Jack) You go sell the cow and bring me back some money.
Farmer:	Hello, Jack. You want to sell your cow?
Jack:	Yes.
Farmer:	Okay, I'll buy it.
Rabbit:	You're supposed to give him some beans.
Farmer:	Here are beans.
Jack:	Mother, I sold the cow and I got beans.
Stepmother:	Beans! I wanted money. Throw them in the garden!
Rabbit:	The beanstalk's supposed to grow.
Beanstalk:	I am growing.
Jack:	(After climbing up the beanstalk) Hello, Giant.

With a little help from the teacher and the prompter, the children continue to act out the story. Jack plays ball with the giant's children and the giant says thank you and gives Jack a golden egg. Then everyone climbs down the beanstalk and has a picnic.

The Role of the Teacher in Fostering Cooperation

Beyond all else, as we look at classrooms in which children have internalized the ideals and values of a cooperative curriculum, we recognize that the teacher, as a model, plays a critical role. When a teacher demonstrates genuine respect and caring, the children learn the value of kindness and reap the rewards of friendship.

The ultimate goal of a cooperative curriculum is to create a classroom environment where every child experiences the joy of having friends, and every child feels wanted, included, and valued.

> I planted a weed in my garden one day.
> It started to grow as if it didn't know
> That a weed has no right to reach up toward the light.
> I went back to the garden, to pluck out the bad seed
> But alas, I couldn't tell which was flower and which weed.